The Goddess of Reason by Mary Johnston

A DRAMA IN FIVE ACTS

Mary Johnston was born on 21st November 1870 in the small town of Buchanan, Virginia, the eldest child of John and Elizabeth Johnston.

During her childhood she was subject to frequent bouts of illness and therefore educated at home with the help of tutors.

When she was 16, her father's work with the Georgia Pacific Railroad meant a move to Birmingham, Alabama. Johnston then attended the Atlanta Female Institute and College of Music in Atlanta, Georgia for three months. This was the only formal education Johnston would receive.

Her mother died in 1889 and she thereafter acted as both her father's companion and as a surrogate mother for her five younger siblings.

Johnston wrote historical books and novels that combined romance with history. Her first book, Prisoners of Hope (1898), dealt with colonial times in Virginia as did her second novel, To Have and to Hold was the best-selling novel of 1900 in the United States. During her long career she wrote across many themes in her 23 novels. She also wrote numerous short stories, two long narrative poems, and one play.

Her 1913 novel 'Hagar' is considered one of the first feminist novels and semi-biographical as it captures the early days of women's rights and her work fighting for women's rights, often at lost commercial opportunities.

Johnston was an early an active member of the Equal Suffrage League of Virginia, which was founded in 1909 by other Richmond-area activists. She chaired it's legislative and lecture committees and served as vice president from 1911 to 1914. Her writings on women's suffrage also appeared in nationally including the Atlantic Monthly.

Mary Johnston died of Bright's disease at her home in Warm Springs, Virginia on 9th May 1936. She was 65 years old and was buried in Hollywood Cemetery in Richmond.

Index of Contents

THE GODDESS OF REASON

DRAMATIS PERSONÆ

René-Amaury de Vardes, Baron of Morbec
Rémond Lalain, Deputy from Vannes
The Abbé Jean de Barbasan
Count Louis de Château-Gui
Captain Fauquemont de Buc
Melipars de L'Orient
Enguerrand La Fôret
The Vidame de Saint-Amour
The Englishman
Grégoire
Raôul the Huntsman
A Sergeant of Hussars
Yvette
The Marquise de Blanchefôret
Mlle. de Château-Gui
Mme. de Vaucourt
Mme. de Malestroit
Mme. de Pont à L'Arche
Sister Fidelis
Sister Simplicia
Sister Benedicta
Nanon
Céleste
Angélique
Séraphine
An Actress
Guests of De Vardes; Peasants; Lackeys; Soldiers; Nuns; Young Girls; The Mob at Nantes; Participants in the Fête of the Goddess of Reason; Republican Commissioners; National Soldiers; Women of the Revolution; Royalist Prisoners; Gaolers; Judges; Executioners; etc., etc.

ACT I

The Château of Morbec in Brittany. A formal garden and a wide terrace with stone balustrade. In the background the château, white and peak-roofed, with great arched doors. Beyond it a distant prospect of a Breton village and of the sea beating against a dangerous coast. To the left a thick wood, to the right a perspective of garden alleys, fountains, and flowering trees. On the terrace a small table set with bread, fruit, and wine. In the angle formed by the level of the terrace and the wide stone steps leading into the garden the statue of a nymph, its high and broad pedestal draped with ivy. Scattered on the terrace and steps a litter of stones, broken cudgels, rusty and uncouth weapons. The sun shines, the trees wave in the wind, the birds sing, the flowers bloom. It is a summer morning in the year 1791.

Enter from one of the garden paths a **LACKEY** and **RÉMOND LALAIN**. **LALAIN** wears a riding dress with a tricolour cockade.

LALAIN
Say to Monsieur the Baron of Morbec,
Rémond Lalain, the Deputy from Vannes,
In haste is riding north, but hath drawn rein—
Hearing to-day of Baron Henri's death—
And audience craves that he may homage pay
To Morbec's latest lord!

THE LACKEY
I go, monsieur!

[Exit **THE LACKEY**.

LALAIN
These gloomy towers!

[He muses as he paces the garden walk before the terrace.

Mirabeau is dead!
Gabriel Riquetti, dead, I salute thee,
Great gladiator! Who treads now the sand
That yesterday was trod by Mirabeau?
Barnave, Lameth, ye are too slight of frame!
There's Lafayette. No, no, mon général!
Robespierre? Go to, thou little man!
Jean Paul Marat, dog leech and People's Friend?
Wild beast to fight with beast! Faugh! Down, Marat!
Who stands this course, why, that man's emperor!
Now how would purple look upon Marat?
Jacques Danton?—Danton! Hot Cordelier!
Dark Titan forging to a Titan's end!
Shake not thy black locks from the tribune there,
Nor rend the heavens with thy mighty voice!
'Tis not for thee, the victor's golden crown,
The voice of France—

[The doors of the château open. Enter **THREE LACKEYS** bearing a great gilt chair, which they place with ceremony at the head of the steps which lead from the terrace into the garden.

FIRST LACKEY [Stamping with his foot upon the terrace]
The gilded chair place here!
We always judge our peasants from this chair,

We lords of Morbec! North terrace, gilt chair!

SECOND LACKEY
Baron Henri sat here the day he died!

FIRST LACKEY
Now Baron René takes his turn!

[They place the chair.

LALAIN [As before]
Danton!
Why not Lalain? It is as good a name!
Mirabeau's dead! Out of my way, Danton!

THIRD LACKEY [Gathering up the stones which lie upon the terrace]
I'll throw these stones into the shrubbery!

SECOND LACKEY [Lifting a rusty scythe from the steps]
This scythe I'll fling into the fountain!

FIRST LACKEY [His hands in his pockets]
Hé!
One sees quite well that we have stood a siege!

[**THE LACKEYS** gather up the stones, the sticks, the broken and rusty tools and weapons.

LALAIN
Where lives the man who doth not worship Might?
O Goddess All-in-All! make me thine own,
4As the bright moon did make Endymion;
And I will rim thy Phrygian cap with stars,
And give thee for thy cestus the tricolour!

[Enter **GRÉGOIRE**.

GRÉGOIRE
Monsieur Lalain!

LALAIN [Waving his hand]
My good Grégoire!

GRÉGOIRE [To the **LACKEYS**]
Despatch!
Monseigneur will be here anon!

[He glances at the stones, etc.

Rubbish!
Away with't!

[Passing the statue of the nymph, he strikes it with his hand.

Will you forever smile?
Stone lips that long have smiled at bitter wrong!
You might, my dear, have lost that smile last night!

FIRST LACKEY
Last night was something like!

SECOND LACKEY [Throwing the stones one by one into the shrubbery]
Sangdieu! last night
My heart was water!

GRÉGOIRE
Ah, poltroon; your heart!

THIRD LACKEY [Making play with a broken stick]
Our baron's a swordsman! His rapier flashed!

FIRST LACKEY
Keen as the blade of the Sieur de Morbec!
—And that is a saying old as the sea!

SECOND LACKEY
Hard as the heart of the Sieur de Morbec!
—And that was said before the sea was made!

[They laugh.

THIRD LACKEY [Pointing to **LALAIN**]
What's he?

GRÉGOIRE
The advocate Rémond Lalain.

THIRD LACKEY
A patriot?

GRÉGOIRE
Hotter than Lanjuinais!

THIRD LACKEY
What does he at Morbec?
How should I know?
His home was once within the village there,

And now and then he visits the curé.

FIRST LACKEY
The curé! He visits Yvette Charruel!

LALAIN [As before]
Mirabeau and I were born in the south.
Oh, the orange flower beside the wall!
And the shaken olives when Mistral wakes!

GRÉGOIRE
Once they were friends, Baron René and he;
The Revolution came between—

FIRST LACKEY [He sends a pike whirling into the shrubbery]
Long live
The Revolution!

GRÉGOIRE
My friend, 'twill live
Without thy bawling!

THIRD LACKEY [Arranging the bottles upon the small table]
So! The red wine here,
The white wine there!
[To a fallen bottle]
Stand up, Aristocrat!

LALAIN
The sun is high!

[He approaches the terrace and addresses the nearest **LACKEY**.

How long must I await
The pleasure of Monsieur the Baron here?

THE LACKEY
Monsieur?

LALAIN
Go, fellow, go! and to him say,
Rémond Lalain—

THE LACKEY
I go, monsieur!

[Exit **THE LACKEY**.

LALAIN
'Tis well,
René de Vardes, to keep me waiting thus!

[**GRÉGOIRE** pours wine into a glass and descending the steps offers it to **LALAIN**.

GRÉGOIRE
The old vintage, Monsieur Lalain!

LALAIN
Thanks, friend.
The day is warm.

[He raises the glass to his lips. Laughter and voices from the winding garden paths.

What's that?

GRÉGOIRE [Shrugging]
More guests, no doubt!
The count, the vidame, and the young marquise!
All Morbihan felicitates Morbec,
And brings our baron bonbons and bouquets,
As if there were no hunger and no frost!

[A distant sound from the wood of harsh and complaining **VOICES**.

LALAIN
And that?

GRÉGOIRE
Soldiers and huntsmen beat the woods;
For half the village is in hiding there,
Having assayed last night to burn Morbec!
As if 'twould burn! This time the soldiers came!
Mon Dieu! the times are bad.

LALAIN [Abruptly]
All the village!
Did Yvette Charruel—

GRÉGOIRE [Shrugging]
Yvette!

FIRST LACKEY [From the terrace]
Yvette!

SECOND LACKEY
I warrant monseigneur will hang Yvette!

[**LALAIN** pours the wine upon the ground and throws the glass from him. It shatters against the balustrade. Laughter and voices. **GUESTS** appear in the garden walks, the **WOMEN** in swelling skirts of silk or muslin, powdered hair and large hats; the **MEN** in brocade and silk with cane swords, or in hunting dress.

A LADY [Curtseying]
Monsieur le Vicomte!

A GENTLEMAN [Bowing]
Madame la Baronne!

MME. DE MALESTROIT
A heavenly day.
Enguerrand La Fôret
No cloud in the sky.

THE VIDAME [Saluting a **GENTLEMAN**]
Count Louis de Château-Gui!

COUNT LOUIS
Ah, monsieur!

[Presents his snuff-box.

For laces I advise Louise. Fichus?
The Bleeding Heart above the flower shop.

THE VIDAME
—A lettre de cachet. To Vincennes he went!

MME. DE MALESTROIT
But ah! what use of laces or fichus!
We emigrate so fast there's none to see!

THE ENGLISHMAN
I quote a great man—my Lord Chesterfield:
"Exist in the unhappy land of France
All signs that history hath ever shown"—

MME. DE PONT À L'ARCHE
The Queen wore carnation, Madame, pale rose,
The Dauphin—

LALAIN
What do I in this galley?
[To **GRÉGOIRE**]
I'll walk aside!

[Exit **LALAIN**.

COUNT LOUIS [To **GRÉGOIRE**]
Was that Rémond Lalain?

GRÉGOIRE
It was, Monsieur le Comte.

COUNT LOUIS
Ah, scélérat!

THE VIDAME
The talked-of Deputy for Vannes?

LA FÔRET
Tribune
Eloquent as Antony!

COUNT LOUIS
Demagogue!

THE ENGLISHMAN
I heard him in the Jacobins. He spoke,
And then they went and tore a palace down!

COUNT LOUIS
Stucco!

[Enter, laughing, **MLLE. DE CHÂTEAU-GUI**, **MELIPARS DE L'ORIENT**, and **CAPTAIN FAUQUEMONT DE BUC**. **DE L'ORIENT** has in his hand a paper of verses.

My daughter and De L'Orient,
Captain Fauquemont de Buc!

MLLE. DE CHÂTEAU-GUI
Messieurs, mesdames!
The poet and his verses!

THE COMPANY
Ah, verses!

COUNT LOUIS
Who is the fair, Monsieur de L'Orient?
Lalage or Laïs or little Fleurette?
Men sang of Célestine when I was young,—
Ah, Célestine, behind thy white rose tree!

DE L'ORIENT
I do not sing of love, Monsieur le Comte!

MLLE. DE CHÂTEAU-GUI
He sings of this day—

DE BUC
The Eve of Saint John.

DE L'ORIENT
It is a Song of Welcome to De Vardes!

DE BUC
But yesterday poor Colonel of Hussars!

MLLE. DE CHÂTEAU-GUI
To-day Monsieur the Baron of Morbec!

DE L'ORIENT
Mars to Bellona leaves the tented field.

DE BUC
That's Bouillé at Metz! Kling! rang our spurs—
De Vardes' and mine—from Verdun to Morbec!

DE L'ORIENT
The warrior hastens to his native weald.

COUNT LOUIS
Would I might see again Henri de Vardes!

DE BUC
It would affright you, sir! The man is dead.

COUNT LOUIS
Ah, while he lived it was as did become
A nobleman of France and Brittany!
He was my friend; together we were young!
From dawn to dusk, from dusk to dawn again,
We searched for pleasure as for buried gold,
And found it, too, in days when we were young!
From every flint we struck the golden sparks,
We plucked the thistle as we plucked the rose,
And battle gave for every star that shone!
O nymphs that laughing fled while we pursued!
O music that was made when we were young!
O gold we won and duels that we fought!

On guard, monsieur, on guard! Sa! sa! A touch!
What shall we drink? Where shall we dine? Ma foi!
There's a melting eye at the Golden Crown!
The Angel pours a Burgundy divine!
Come, come, the quarrel's o'er! So, arm in arm!
O worlds we lost and won when we were young!
O lips we kissed within the jasmine bower!
O sirens singing in the clear moonlight!—
With Bacchus we drank, with Apollo loved,
With Actæon hunted when we were young!
The wax-lights burned with softer lustre then.
The music was more rich when we were young.
Violet was the perfume for hair powder,
Ruffles were point and buckles were brilliant
And lords were lords in the old land of France!
We did what we would, and lettres de cachet,
Like cooing doves they fluttered from our hands!

DE L'ORIENT
Our tribute take, last of a noble line!

COUNT LOUIS
Women! There will come no more such women!

DE L'ORIENT
The laurel and the empress rose we twine.

COUNT LOUIS
And Henri's gone! And now his cousin reigns,—
René de Vardes that hath been years away!
The King is dead. Well, well, long live the King!
They say he's brave as Crillon, handsome too,
With that bel air that no De Vardes's without!

[Enter **MME. DE VAUCOURT** followed by **THE ABBÉ** Jean de Barbasan.

MLLE. DE CHÂTEAU-GUI
Monsieur l'Abbé!

DE BUC
Madame de Vaucourt!

MME. DE VAUCOURT [With outspread hands]
You've heard? Last night they strove to burn Morbec!

ALL
What?

MME. DE VAUCOURT
The peasants!

COUNT LOUIS
Again!

DE BUC
Ah, I am vexed.
Messieurs, mesdames, the Baron of Morbec
Silence enjoined, or the tale I'd have told!
The abbé is so bold—

THE ABBÉ
De Buc's so proud!
And just because he brought us help from Vannes!
The red Hussars to hive the bees again!

THE ENGLISHMAN
The seigneur and his peasants are at odds?

THE ABBÉ
Slightly!

COUNT LOUIS [Complacently]
Henri was hated! Hate descends
With the land.

DE L'ORIENT
There is a girl of these parts—

COUNT LOUIS
Eh?

DE L'ORIENT
She plays the firebrand.

COUNT LOUIS
Bah!

DE L'ORIENT
She hath
The loveliest face!

COUNT LOUIS
Hm!

THE ABBÉ
I am unscathed.

De Vardes is slightly wounded!

ALL
Oh!

COUNT LOUIS
Morbleu!
And how did it happen, Monsieur l'Abbé?

THE ABBÉ
Behold us at our ease in the great hall,
De Vardes and I, a-musing o'er piquet!
Voltaire beside us, for we read "Alzire,"
A wine as well, more suave than any verse;
A still and starlit night, soft, fair, and warm;
Wax-lights, and roses in a china bowl.
He laid aside his sword and I my cap,
All tranquilly at home, the Two Estates!
He held carte blanche, I followed with quatorze.
The roses sweetly smelled, the candles burned,
At peace we were with nature and mankind.—
A crash of painted glass! a whirling stone!
A candle out! the roses all o'erturned!
The thunder of a log against our doors!
A clattering of sabots! a sudden shout!
Morbec, Morbec, it is thy Judgment Night!
Admission, admission, Aristocrats!
Red turns the night, the servants all rush in.
Sieur! Sieur! the lackeys moan and wring their hands.
Give, give! the terrace croaks. Burn, Morbec, burn!
The great bell swings in the windy tower
Till the wolves in the forest pause to hear.
Fall, Morbec, fall! France has no need of thee!
Upsprings a rosy light! a smell of smoke!
Mischief's afoot! The Baron of Morbec
Lays down his cards and takes his rapier up,
Hums Le Sein de sa Famille, shuts Alzire,
Resignedly rises—

COUNT LOUIS [Rubbing his hands]
Expresses regret
That monsieur his guest—

THE ABBÉ
Should be incommoded
And turns to the door. I levy the tongs.
The seneschal Grégoire hauls from the wall
An ancient arquebus! The lackeys wail,

And nothing do, as is the lackey's wont!
Again the peasants thunder at the door!
Open, De Vardes! Oh, hated of all names!
The new is as the old! Death to De Vardes!
The log strikes full, and now a panel breaks;
In comes a hand that brandishes a pike;
A voice behind, We've come to sup with thee!
For thou hast bread and we have none, De Vardes!

THE ENGLISHMAN
Ha, ha! ha, ha! ha, ha!

COUNT LOUIS
You laugh, monsieur?

THE ABBÉ
I like calmness myself. Calm of the sea,
Calm skies, the calm spring, and calmness of mind!
A tempest's plebeian! So I admired
René de Vardes when he walked to the door
And opened it! Behold the whole wolf pack,
As lean as 'twere winter! canaille all!
Sans-culottes and tatterdemalions,
Mere dust of the field and sand of the shore;
Humanity's shreds would follow the mode,
And burn the château of their rightful lord!
De Vardes' peasants in fine. Mort aux tyrans!
À bas Aristocrat! Vive la patrie!
Vive la Révolution! In they pressed,
Gaunt, haggard, and shrill, and full in the front—
Young and fair, conceive! dark-eyed and red-lipped—
A fury, a mænad, a girl called—

DE L'ORIENT
Yvette!

THE ABBÉ
So they named her, the peasants of Morbec,
Named and applauded the dark-eyed besom!
When, De Vardes' drawn rapier just touching
Her breast-knot of blue as she stood in his path,
Up went her brown hand, armed with a sickle!—
De Vardes is a known fencer,—'tis lucky!
His wound is not deep, and in the left arm!

THE VIDAME
She may hang for that! How high I forget
The gallows should be—

COUNT LOUIS [Offering his snuff-box]
Monsieur le Vidame,
Thirty feet, I believe!

THE VIDAME
But not in chains—

COUNT LOUIS
No! It was the left arm.

DE L'ORIENT
What did De Vardes?

THE ABBÉ
De Vardes, with Liancourt and Rochefoucauld,
Holds that the peasant doth possess a soul!
I think it hurt him to the heart that he,
New come to Morbec, and unknown to these,
His vassals of the village, field, and shore,
Should be esteemed by them an enemy,
A Baron Henri come again, forsooth!
But since 'twas so, out rapier! parry! thrust!
Diable! he's a swordsman to my mind!
The mænad with the sickle he puts by;
Runs through the arm a clamourer of corvée,
Brings howling to his knees a sans-culotte,
And strikes a flail from out a claw-like hand!
They falter, they give way, the craven throng!
The women cry them on; they swarm again.
His bright steel flashes, rise and fall my tongs!
But the lackeys are naught, and Grégoire finds
A flaw in his musket; he will not fire!
Pardieu! the things this Revolution kills!
There is no faithfulness in service now!
Our peasants grow bold. Ma foi! we're at bay!
De Vardes and De Barbasan, rapier, tongs!
Wild blows and wild cries, blown smoke and a glare,
And the girl Yvette with her reaping hook
Still pushed to the front by the women there!
Upon De Vardes' white sleeve the blood is dark,
And his breath comes fast! I see the event
As 'twill look in print in Paris next week,
In L'Ami du Peuple or Journal du Roi!
"The Vain Defence of an Ancient Château!
When we Burn so Much, why not Burn the Land?"
And I break with my tongs a young death's-head
That's bawling—What think you?—Vive la République.

COUNT LOUIS
Death and damnation!

THE ABBÉ
So I said! And then,
Quite, I assure you, in time's very nick,
The saint De Vardes prays to smiled on him!
A thunder clap!—Pas de charge! En avant!
Captain Fauquemont de Buc and his Hussars!

DE BUC
Warned by the saint, we galloped from Auray!

THE ABBÉ
Like the dead leaves borne afar on the blast,
Or like the sea mist when the sun rises,
Or like the red deer when the horn's sounded,—
Like anything in short that's light o' heel,—
Vanished our peasants! The women went last;
And last of all the mænad with the eyes!
Jesu! She might have been Jeanne d'Arc, that girl!
The man who captures her has a hand full!—
To the deep woods they fled, are hunted now.—
De Vardes and I gave welcome to De Buc,
Put out the fire, attended to our wounds,
Resumed our cards, and finished our Alzire—
The Château of Morbec stands, you observe!

[The **COMPANY** applauds.

MLLE. DE CHÂTEAU-GUI
But who was the saint?—

DE BUC
Ah, here is De Vardes!

[Enter **DE VARDES**. He is dressed in slight mourning and carries his arm in a sling.

THE GUESTS
Monsieur the Baron of Morbec!

DE VARDES
Welcome,
The brave and the fair, my old friends and new!
Welcome to Morbec!

COUNT LOUIS

Ah, your wounded arm!—
Our regret is profound!

DE VARDES
It is nothing.
The fraternal embrace of the people!

COUNT LOUIS
Oh, the people!

MME. DE VAUCOURT
The people!

DE L'ORIENT
The people!

COUNT LOUIS
My friend, permit us to hope you will make
Of the people a signal example!

DE VARDES
They are misguided.

COUNT LOUIS
Misguided! Morbleu!

DE VARDES
I will talk to them.

COUNT LOUIS
Monsieur le Baron,
Let your soldiers talk with a bayonet's point,
Your bailiffs with a rope—

MME. DE VAUCOURT
But what good saint
Brought warning to Auray?

DE L'ORIENT
I guess that saint!

[**A LACKEY** appears upon the terrace.

THE LACKEY
Madame la Marquise de Blanchefôret!

THE GUESTS
Ah!

La belle marquise!

[Enter **THE MARQUISE**.

DE BUC
The saint!

DE VARDES
My neighbour fair,
And to De Barbasan and me last night
A guardian angel—

[He greets **THE MARQUISE**.

Madame la Marquise!

THE MARQUISE
Monsieur le Baron!
[To the **COMPANY**]
Messieurs, mesdames!

DE VARDES
From Blanchefôret to Auray through the night
This lady rode—

THE MARQUISE [With gayety]
Ah, how I rode last night,
To Auray through the dark! This way it was:
I overheard two peasants yestereve
As in a lane I sought for eglantine.
"How long hath Morbec stood?" said one. "Too long!
But when to-morrow dawns 'twill not be there!
And we were born, I think, to burn châteaux!—
Ten, by the village clock—forget it not!"

THE ABBÉ
Ah, ay, the while I dealt the clock struck ten.

THE MARQUISE
It was already dusk.—Like grey death moths
They slipped away! I knew not whom to trust,
For in these times there's no fidelity,
No faithful groom, no steadfast messenger!
My little page brought me my Zuleika.
I knew the red Hussars were at Auray,
And that 'twas said they loved their colonel well!
So to Auray came Zuleika and I!

DE BUC
We thought it was Dian in huntress dress!

DE VARDES
How deeply am I, Goddess, in thy debt!
No gold is coined wherewith I may repay!

[Music within.

THE MARQUISE
Give me a rose from yonder tree!

[Laughing **VOICES** within.

MLLE. DE CHÂTEAU-GUI
More guests,
They're on the south terrace!

DE L'ORIENT
Violins too!
Ah, the old air—

[He sings.

There lived a king in Ys,
In Ys the city old!
Beside the sounding sea
He counted o'er his gold.

DE VARDES
Let us meet them.

[He gives his hand to **THE MARQUISE**. Exeunt.

[**COUNT LOUIS**, **THE ABBÉ**, **DE BUC**, **DE L'ORIENT**, etc. **GRÉGOIRE** approaches **DE VARDES**.

GRÉGOIRE
Monseigneur—Monsieur the Deputy!

DE VARDES
Ah!
Say to monsieur I'm not at leisure now.

[Exeunt **DE VARDES** and **THE MARQUISE**. The terrace and garden are deserted save for **GRÉGOIRE**, who seats himself in the shadow of the balustrade.

GRÉGOIRE
Humph!—Monseigneur's not at leisure.

[He draws a Paris journal from his pocket and reads, following the letters with his forefinger.

What news?
What says Jean Paul Marat, the People's Friend?

[A cry from the wood and the sound of breaking boughs. **YVETTE** and **SÉRAPHINE** enter the garden. Raôul the **HUNTSMAN'S** voice within.

THE HUNTSMAN
Hilloa!—Hilloa!—Hilloa!

[**YVETTE** and **SÉRAPHINE** turn towards one of the garden alleys. Laughter and voices.

YVETTE
Go not that way!

SÉRAPHINE
There is no way!

THE HUNTSMAN [Within]
Hilloa!—Hilloa!

SÉRAPHINE
We're caught!

YVETTE
The terrace there! Behind the stone woman!

[They cross the garden to the terrace.

SÉRAPHINE [She stops abruptly and points to the table]
Bread!

THE HUNTSMAN [Nearer]
Hilloa!—Hilloa!

[**YVETTE** and **SÉRAPHINE** turn from the table and hide behind the tall, ivy-draped pedestal of the statue. **GRÉGOIRE** looks up from his paper and sees them.

[Enter Raôul **THE HUNTSMAN**.

THE HUNTSMAN
This way they came!

GRÉGOIRE [Jerking his thumb over his shoulder]
Down yonder path!—plump to the woods again!

THE HUNTSMAN
The Hussars from Auray have twenty rogues!

GRÉGOIRE
Indeed!

THE HUNTSMAN
These two and my bag's full!

[Exit **THE HUNTSMAN**.

GRÉGOIRE
Diable!
[He reads aloud.
Weary at last of intolerable wrong,
The peasants of Goy in Normandy rose
And burned the château. Who questions their right?

[He folds his paper.

Saint Yves! this stone is much harder than Goy!

[He looks fixedly at the statue and raises his voice.

Ma'm'selle who would smile at the trump of doom,
I think that all the village will be hanged!
And at its head that brown young witch they call
Yvette—

[Re-enter **DE VARDES** and **THE MARQUISE**.

DE VARDES [To **GRÉGOIRE**]
Begone!

[Exit **GRÉGOIRE**. **DE VARDES** and **THE MARQUISE** rest beside the statue, **YVETTE** listening.

Why, what's a soldier for?
But pity me, pity me, belle Marquise!
Since pity is so sweet!

THE MARQUISE
I'm sure it is
A fearful wound!

DE VARDES
A fearful wound indeed!
But 'tis not in the arm!

THE MARQUISE
No, monsieur?

DE VARDES
No!
The heart! I swear that it is bleeding fast!
And I have naught wherewith to stanch the wound.
Your kerchief—

THE MARQUISE
Just a piece of lace!

DE VARDES
'Twill serve.

THE MARQUISE [Giving her handkerchief]
Well, there!—Now tell me of last night.

DE VARDES
Last night!
Why, all this tintamarre was but a dream,
Fanfare of fairy trumpets while we slept.
A night it was for love-in-idleness,
And fragrant thoughts and airy phantasy!
There was no moon, but Venus shone as bright;
The honeysuckle blew its tiny horn
To tell the rose a moth was coming by.
Clarice-Marie! sang all the nightingales,
Or would have sung were nightingales abroad!
Hush, hush! the little waves kept whispering.
The ivy at your window still was peeping;
You lay in dreams, that gold curl on your breast!

THE MARQUISE
No, no! You cheat me not, monsieur! Last night
I did not sleep!

DE VARDES
Nor I!

THE MARQUISE
Miserable brigands!

DE VARDES
No, not brigands! Just wretched flesh and blood.

THE MARQUISE
You pity them?

DE VARDES
Ay.

THE MARQUISE
Were I a seigneur,
Lord of Morbec—

DE VARDES
Were I a poor fisher,
Sailing at sunrise home from the islands,
Over the sea, and all my heart singing!
And you were a herd girl slender and sweet,
With the gold of your hair beneath your cap,
And you kept the cows and you were my douce,
And you waved your hand from the green cliff head
When the sun and I came up from the sea!—
And there was a seigneur so great and grim
Who walked in his garden and said aloud,
"How many fish has he taken for me?
Which of her cows shall I keep for myself?
I leave him enough to pay for the Mass
The day he is drowned, and the girl shall have
The range of the hills for her one poor cow!
Why should the fisher fret, the herd girl weep?
There is no reason in a serf's dull heart!
I might have taken all. It is my right!"
La belle Marquise, what would the herd girl do?
And should the fisher suffer and say naught?

THE MARQUISE
There is no fisher nor no herd girl here.
How fair the roses of Morbec, monsieur!

DE VARDES
Ay, they are lovely queens. They know it too!
I better like the heartsease at your feet.

THE MARQUISE
It is a peasant flower!—Sieur de Morbec,
Have you never loved?

DE VARDES
How fair is the day!
For loving how fit! 'Tis the Eve of Saint John.

THE MARQUISE
Yes.

DE VARDES
Last year I loved on this very day.
Take the omen, madame!

THE MARQUISE
We had not met,
You and I!

DE VARDES
Ah, 'tis true! We had not met!—
And so, fair as you are, you were not there,
In Paimpont Wood, on the Eve of Saint John?

THE MARQUISE
No!

DE VARDES
I wonder who was!

THE MARQUISE
In Paimpont Wood!
It is haunted!

DE VARDES
On the Eve of Saint John
I rode from Morbec here to Chatillon,
And through the wood of Paimpont fared alone.
It is a forest where enchantments thrive,
And a fair dream doth drop from every tree!
The old, old world of bitterness and strife
Is remote as winter, remote as death.
It was high noon in the turbulent town;
But clocks never strike in the elfin wood,
And the sun's ruddy gold is elsewhere spent.
The light was dim in the depths of Paimpont,
Green, reverend, and dim as the light may be
In a sea king's palace under the sea.
The wind did not blow; the flowering bough
Was still as the rose on a dead man's breast.
On velvet hoof the doe and fawn went by;
In other woods the lark and linnet sang;
A stealthy way was taken by the fox;
The badger trod upon the softest moss;
And like a shadow flitted past the hare.
Without a sound the haunted fountain played.
The oak boughs dreamed; the pine was motionless;
Its silver arms the beech in silence spread;

The poplar had forgot its lullaby.
It was as still as cloudland in the wood,
For in a hawthorn brake old Merlin sleeps,
And every leaf is hushed for love of him.
There through the years they sleep and listless dream,
The wood of Paimpont and the wizard old.
They dream of valleys where the lilies blow;
They dream of woodland gods and castles high,
Of faun and Pan and of the Table Round,
Of dryad trees and of a maiden dark—
That Vivien whom old Merlin once did love,
Vivien le Gai whose love was poisonous!

THE MARQUISE
I've heard it said by women spinning flax,
"Who wanders in Paimpont wanders in love;
Let him who loves in Paimpont Wood beware!"

DE VARDES
Ah, idle word! Oh, many silver bells
Since Vivien's day have rung, Beware, beware!
And rung in vain, for in every clime
Lies Paimpont Wood, dawns the Eve of Saint John!

THE MARQUISE
And in the forest there whom did you love?

DE VARDES
I do not know. I have not seen her since,
Unless—unless I saw her face last night!

YVETTE [Behind the base of the statue]
Oh!—

DE VARDES
Did you not hear a voice?

THE MARQUISE
'Tis the wind.—
You're riding through the wood to Chatillon.

DE VARDES
It was a lonely forest, deep and vast,
A secret and a soundless trysting-place,
Where one might meet, nor be surprised to meet,
From out his past, or from his life to come,
A veilèd shape, a presence bitter-sweet,
A thing that was, a thing was yet to be!

It seemed a fatal place, a destined day.
Down a long aisle of beechen trees I rode,
And came upon a small and sunny vale,
And there I met a face from out a dream,
An ancient dream, a dark and lovely face.—
Give me your fan of pearl and ivory!

[He takes the fan from **THE MARQUISE**.

I'll turn enchanter, use it for my rod,
And make you see, Marquise, the very place!

[He points with the fan.

Here sprang the silver column of a beech;
There, mossy knees of a most ancient oak;
Yonder a wall of thickest foliage rose;
And here a misty streamlet flowed
With a voice more low than the dying fall
Of a trouvère's lute in Languedoc,
And on its shore the slender flowers grew;
Upon a foxglove bell hung papillon;
And all around the grass was long and fine.
Within this sylvan space, ah, ages since!
The white-robed Druids in the cold moonlight
Had reared an altar stone of wondrous height;
The fane was there, the Druids were away.
All fragrant was the air, and sunny still,—
On the Eve of Saint John 'tis ever so!
Above, the sky was blue without a cloud;
The sun stood sentinel o'er the haunted wood.
And there she lay, the woman of a dream,
Against the Druid Stone, amid the bloom;
Her eyes were on the stream; she leaned her ear;
From far away the trouvère played to her;
In flakes of gold the sunlight blessed her hair;
Her lips were red; she seemed a princess old;
Mid purple bloom she lay and gazed afar,
In the magic wood on a magic day,
Listening to hear the mighty trouvère play.
Was she a princess or a peasant maid?
I do not know, pardie! She may have been
That Vivien who wrought old Merlin wrong.
I cannot tell if she were rich or poor;
I only saw her face; I only know
I loved the dream I met in Paimpont Wood
As I did ride last year to Chatillon
On Saint John's Eve.—

[He lays the fan upon the table.

So I have loved, Marquise!

THE MARQUISE
What did your pretty dream?

DE VARDES
As other dreams;
She fled!

THE MARQUISE
And you pursued?

DE VARDES
Yes, but in vain!
Trouble no dream that is dreamed in Paimpont!
The wood closed around her; she vanished quite.
It must have been that evil Vivien,
Since you, Marquise, have never trod the wood!

THE MARQUISE
Would I have fled?

DE VARDES
Why, then, without doubt
It was Vivien! But yet do you know
'Tis the Eve of Saint John, and here, last night,
I dreamed that I saw my dream again!

[The hand and arm of the statue fall, broken, to the ground at the feet of **THE MARQUISE**.

THE MARQUISE
Ah!

DE VARDES [Pushes the marble aside with his foot]
It is nothing! The stone was cracked last night.
Some crack-brained peasant had no better mark!

THE MARQUISE
'Tis a présigne!—I feel it.—

DE VARDES
You shudder!

THE MARQUISE
One trod near my grave! I'm suddenly cold!

DE VARDES
The sun never shines on this terrace!

THE MARQUISE
No!
'Twas an air from the Forest of Paimpont
Came over me!

[**VOICES** within. **DE L'ORIENT** sings.

DE L'ORIENT
In Ys they did rejoice,
In Ys the wine was free;
The Ocean lent its voice
Unto that revelry!

THE MARQUISE
Oh, come away!
Let us find the violins and the sun!
There are other woods than Paimpont. Come away!

[Exeunt **DE VARDES** and **THE MARQUISE**.

YVETTE [Leaves the shadow of the statue]
'Twas he! That horseman who did waken me
That Saint John's Eve I strayed in Paimpont Wood!
O Our Lady—

SÉRAPHINE [From the statue]
Saint Yves! There is bread!

[**YVETTE** takes from the table a loaf of bread and throws it to **SÉRAPHINE**, who springs upon it like a famished wolf.

SÉRAPHINE [Setting her teeth in the loaf]
Ah—h—h!

[**YVETTE**, about to lay her hand upon another round of bread, sees the fan lying upon the cloth. She leaves the bread and takes up the fan. It opens in her hand.

YVETTE
Oh!—

[She sits in the great chair and waves the fan slowly to and fro.

Were I a lady fair and free,
I would powder my hair with dust of gold,

I would clasp a necklace around my throat,
Of jewels rare, and a gown I would wear,
Blue silk like Our Lady of Toute Remède!
My shoes should be made of golden stuff,
And a broidered glove should dress my hand,
My hand so white that a lord might kiss!
I would spin fine flax from a silver wheel,
I would weave a web for my bridal sheets,
I would sing of King Gradlon under the sea,
Were I a lady fair and free!

[Enter **GRÉGOIRE**.

SÉRAPHINE [From the statue]
Yvette!
Yvette!
Yvette
Peace, peace!

GRÉGOIRE
What have you there?

YVETTE
A fan.
So long I've wanted one!

GRÉGOIRE
A fan, forsooth!
You cannot eat a fan, drink it, wear it!

YVETTE
I would look on't.
One day at Vannes the deputy's sister
Showed me a fan, but it was not like this!
Oh, not like this with these wreaths of roses,
These painted clouds, this fairy ship!

GRÉGOIRE
The price
Would keep a peasant from starvation!
And belike it fell from the lifted hand
Of Madame la Marquise de Blanchefôret!

[The fan breaks in **YVETTE'S** hand.

SÉRAPHINE [Leaving the statue]
Thou evil-starred!

YVETTE
What have I done?

GRÉGOIRE
Diantre!
Now you will be beaten as well as hanged!

YVETTE
She called us miserable brigands!

[Enter **DE VARDES**.

SÉRAPHINE
Saint Yves! Saint Hervé! Saint Herbot!

DE VARDES [To **GRÉGOIRE**]
Voices?

GRÉGOIRE
Monseigneur?

DE VARDES
The fan of Madame la Marquise.

GRÉGOIRE
Monseigneur?

DE VARDES [Perceiving **YVETTE** and **SÉRAPHINE**]
What will you have, good people?

SÉRAPHINE
Saint Guenolé! Saint Thromeur! Saint Sulic!—
He did not see us in the dark last night!

[**DE VARDES** regards them more closely.

GRÉGOIRE
Séraphine Robin—Yvette Charruel—
They are not bad folk, monseigneur!

SÉRAPHINE
No, faith!

[**DE VARDES** studies the name written upon a playing card which he holds in his hand.

DE VARDES [To **GRÉGOIRE**]
Say to Monsieur the Deputy from Vannes
That I await him here.

[Exit **GRÉGOIRE**. **DE VARDES** looks intently at **YVETTE**.

YVETTE
It was so beautiful,
The fan—I took it in my hand—it broke!

SÉRAPHINE
All that she touches breaks!

DE VARDES [To **YVETTE**]
Wast ever thou
In the Forest of Paimpont?

YVETTE
Oh, monseigneur!
Last Eve of Saint John, by the Druid Stone!

DE VARDES
Ah!—

[He takes the fan from **YVETTE**'s hand and examines it.

Beyond all remedy!—Well, 'tis done.
Do not tremble so!

YVETTE
I tremble not!

[Enter **LALAIN**.

SÉRAPHINE [To **YVETTE**]
Here's Monsieur Lalain!

YVETTE
I care not, I!

DE VARDES
Ah,
Rémond Lalain!

LALAIN [Stiffly]
Monsieur—

DE VARDES
A moment, pray,
Until I've spoken with these worthy folk!

LALAIN [Coldly]
Monsieur the Baron's pleasure!

[He moves aside, but in passing speaks to **YVETTE**.

Yvette! Yvette!

YVETTE
Monsieur the Deputy?

LALAIN
Too fair art thou!
Beware! This is the Seigneur of Morbec!

YVETTE
I know.

LALAIN
He is the foe of France!

YVETTE
I know.

DE VARDES [To **SÉRAPHINE**]
Your business, well?

SÉRAPHINE [Stammering]
Our business, monseigneur?—
Oh, give me help, Saint Yves le Véridique!—
Our business?—Saint Michel!—Well, since we're here!—
Monseigneur, was the pullet plump and sweet?

DE VARDES
The pullet?

YVETTE
Our pullet, monseigneur.

LALAIN
Distrained for rent!

SÉRAPHINE
And Lisette, monseigneur?
May we enquire for Lisette's health?

DE VARDES
Lisette?

YVETTE
Our cow, monseigneur.

LALAIN
Taken for taxes!

SÉRAPHINE
It was the best Lisette!

YVETTE
She followed me
Through the green lanes, and o'er the meadows salt.
Her breath was sweet as May!

DE VARDES
It would please you
To have your cow again?

YVETTE
Oh, monseigneur!
Monseigneur, I'm the herd girl of Morbec!

LALAIN [Aside]
They gaze into each other's eyes!

DE VARDES
What is
Thy name?

YVETTE
Yvette.

SÉRAPHINE
Ay, ay, 'tis so!—Yvette.
Called also The Right of the Seigneur!—

DE VARDES
The Right of the Seigneur!

SÉRAPHINE [Nodding]
Just so.

LALAIN [Aside]
Recall
Just one of a great seigneur's privileges!
Baiser des mariées, in short, my friend!

SÉRAPHINE

O holy Saints! the night that she was born!
The thunder pealed, the sea gave forth a cry,
The forked lightnings played, the winds were out
And in the hut her mother lay and wailed,
And called on all the saints, the while Jehan
(That was her mother's husband, Monseigneur),
He stood and struck his heel against the logs.
Up flew the sparks, for all the wood was drift,
Salt with the sea, and every flame was blue.
I held the babe—Yvette, show monseigneur
The mark beneath the ear!

YVETTE
No!

SÉRAPHINE
Stubbornness!
'Tis there!

LALAIN
A birthmark—a small blue flower!

DE VARDES
Ah!

SÉRAPHINE
Ay! a little mark.—Jehan Charruel!
He was a violent man,—the sea breeds such!
He cursed Yvonne upon her pallet there,
So pale she was, and dying with the tide!
He cursed the saints, the purple mark, the babe,
And some one else I dare not name—

LALAIN
I dare!
Henri-Etienne-Amaury de Vardes,
Late Baron of Morbec!

SÉRAPHINE
Then out he goes,
A-weeping hard—Jehan—into the night.
Ouf! how it blew!—
The sea ran high, he met it in the dark,
Was drowned! Yvonne went with the ebb. Behold Yvette!

[**SÉRAPHINE** retreats to the table, where she furtively drinks from a half-emptied wineglass. **LALAIN** follows her and the two talk together.

DE VARDES
That purple flower, that violet
By nature limned upon thy slender throat,—
From north to south, from east to west 'tis known!
A De Vardes bore that mark at Poitiers.
The marshal, Hugues the Fair, and black Arnaud,
The late baron—Why, what hast thou to do
With burning down châteaux to make a light
To show the Morbihan that purple flower?

YVETTE
O Our Lady of Thorns!

DE VARDES
Herd girl too fair!
And vision of Paimpont, fair as I dreamed!
How fair was thy errand last night?

YVETTE
Monseigneur!

DE VARDES
In the ashes of Morbec what shouldst thou find?

YVETTE
We only wished to make a little light—
A little light to let the neighbours know
That we were hungry!

DE VARDES
What neighbours hast thou?

YVETTE
Normandy and Maine, Anjou and Poitou,
The sea, the sky, and somewhat far away,
The Club of the Jacobins at Paris.

DE VARDES
Thy father was a nobleman of France!

YVETTE
I never had a father, monseigneur!
I had a mother, and she loved, they say,
She dearly loved the fisherman Jehan!
When for the dead I pray, I pray for them.

DE VARDES
How old art thou?

YVETTE
How old? Ah, let me see!

[She counts upon her fingers.

The year the hailstones fell and killed the wheat;
The year the flax failed and we made no songs;
The year I begged for bread; the bitter year
We buried Louison who died of cold,
And Jacques was hanged who shot the seigneur's deer;
The Pardon of Sainte Anne I had a gown;
Came Angélique from Paris, told us how
The wicked Queen was smiling, smiling there;
Justine pined away, they shot Michel If,
Down fell the Bastille, I learned Ça ira;
The deputy came to the curé's house,
Beside the deep blue sea I walked with him.
A day there was at Vannes, a glorious day,
When music played, and every banner waved,
And all the folk went mad and rang the bells!
Vive la Révolution! Vive Mirabeau!
Vive Rémond Lalain! I wept when 'twas o'er,
Last summer was so fair! I wandered far,
One day I wandered through a darksome wood—
'Twas on the Eve of good Saint John, I know!

DE VARDES
Ah—

YVETTE
The summer fled, the light, the warmth did go,
The winter came that was so cruel cold,
Cold as the dead! And hunger, monseigneur,
With bread at the château!—Died Baron Henri.—
The summer came again, the roses bloomed,
The roses bloomed, but they were not for us!
For us the dank seaweed, the thorny furze.
The lark sang well, but ah, it sang too high!
We could not lift our hearts to heaven's gate;
We only heard the wind moan at our door.
We cried to the saints, but they took no heed!
One told us what they did at Goy and Vannes,
At Goy and Vannes, pardieu! they helped themselves!
We heard there had come a new lord to Morbec,
A soldier and a stranger to us all!
Three days have gone since I did sit alone
Upon the cliff edge in the waving grass;

The mew and curlew cried, the night wind blew,
And in the sunset glow red turned Morbec!
I thought of my mother, I thought of France,
I looked at the château cruel and high,
And as I was hungry I ate my black bread!—
I think, monseigneur, that I am nineteen.

DE VARDES
Pauvre petite!

YVETTE
Ah, poor indeed!

DE VARDES
How dark
Thine eyes!

YVETTE
My mother's were darker, they say!

DE VARDES
Thy face is the face of a picture there.

YVETTE
I know—the Duchess Jeannc, who died for love.

DE VARDES
Did Vivien teach thee magic in the wood?

YVETTE
Monseigneur?

DE VARDES
Pauvre petite!

YVETTE
O Our Lady!
The roses smell so sweet—

[**LALAIN** comes forward.

LALAIN
I pardon crave,
But I must sup to-night at Rennes. Please you,
Release this peasant girl! Affairs there are
Of which I'd speak—

DE VARDES

Ay, presently!

LALAIN
Now!

DE VARDES
Monsieur!

LALAIN
Citoyen René-Amaury Vardes—

DE VARDES
Is that, monsieur, the latest Paris mode?
Citoyen René-Amaury Vardes,
The De left off, our hats [Glances at **LALAIN**] left on!

LALAIN [Removing his hat]
Monsieur
The Baron of Morbec!

DE VARDES [Bowing]
Monsieur
The Deputy for Vannes!

[Laughter and voices within.

[Enter from the château **THE MARQUISE** and **MLLE. DE CHÂTEAU-GUI** with **DE L'ORIENT** and **DE BUC**.

DE L'ORIENT [Sings]
Then spake the king of Ys
Above the song and shout,
Bring here the golden key
That keeps the ocean out!

THE MARQUISE
Monsieur le Baron,
My lost fan!

YVETTE [Aside]
Oh me!

DE VARDES
Madame la Marquise,
I will give you a fan that's to my taste;
By Watteau painted, mounted by Laudet,
Fragile and fine, an Adonis of fans!
This that I broke I will keep for myself.

[Pockets the fan.

Forgive the mere accident!

YVETTE
Ah!

SÉRAPHINE [From the table]
Ah—h—h!

LALAIN [Aside]
Gods!
If I forgive!

THE MARQUISE
At Blanchefôret, monsieur,
The Watteau, Laudet, Adonis of fans,
I'll take from your hand—

DE VARDES
I ride there anon,
[Aside]
But not through the Forest of Paimpont
And not on the Eve of Saint John.

THE MARQUISE
Come soon,
My garden is sweetest in June.

DE L'ORIENT [Sings]
In Ys they sing no more,
In Ys the city old!
The waves are rolling o'er
The king and all his gold.

MLLE. DE CHÂTEAU-GUI
Look at my fan, Monsieur le Baron!

[**LALAIN** crosses to **YVETTE**.

LALAIN
Hast thou forgot, hast thou forgot, Yvette,
Thy part, thy lot, the very name they give thee?
This is Morbec, this is the brazen castle!
There are no roses here.

YVETTE
So generous

He was!

LALAIN
Generous! Oh, well are you called
The Right of the Seigneur!

YVETTE [Passionately]
Give me not that
Detestable name!

LALAIN
So meek under wrongs—

YVETTE
Oh!

LALAIN
So quick to forget—

YVETTE
Oh!

LALAIN
La patrie—
Sworn oaths—the tricolour—

YVETTE
Anger me not!

LALAIN
On your lips Ça Ira! but in your heart
O Richard, O mon Roi!

YVETTE
'Tis false!

LALAIN
And I—and I—Yvette!

YVETTE
Speak not to me!

LALAIN
You gaze at that man! I tell you he wooes
Madame la Marquise de Blanchefôret!

[**YVETTE** crosses to **THE MARQUISE**, **DE VARDES**, and the **GUESTS**.

YVETTE [To **THE MARQUISE**]
Madame!
I broke the fan! I would pay if I might.
I would keep your cows, or spin your flax—

THE MARQUISE
The fan!
You broke the fan—not monsieur there!

YVETTE
No, I!

THE MARQUISE
Sainte Geneviève!

[Enter **COUNT LOUIS**, **THE VIDAME**, **MME. DE VAUCOURT**, etc.

SÉRAPHINE
Yvette!

Count Louis
La belle Marquise!

[**SÉRAPHINE** draws **YVETTE** back to the base of the statue. Count Louis, **THE MARQUISE**, and the guests talk together. **LALAIN** crosses to **DE VARDES**.

LALAIN
René de Vardes!

DE VARDES
Rémond Lalain!

LALAIN
This day I bury our friendship of old!

DE VARDES
So!

LALAIN
I owe to you a thousand louis
Which I'll repay, monsieur!

DE VARDES
I doubt it not.

LALAIN
Touch not the girl Yvette!

DE VARDES
At last the heart of the matter! I see
You have been through the Forest of Paimpont.

LALAIN
Or touch at your peril!

DE VARDES
Monsieur!

LALAIN
Oh, if
You lay your hand upon your sword, monsieur,
I'm for you there!

DE VARDES
Art mad, or drunk with power,
Monsieur the favourite of the Jacobins?

LALAIN
There'll come a day when to be Jacobin
Is something more, monsieur, than to be king!

DE VARDES
Indeed!

[A **SERGEANT** of Hussars appears on the terrace and salutes.
Sergeant!

THE SERGEANT
My Colonel!

DE VARDES
Well, your report.

THE SERGEANT
My Colonel, wood and shore we've searched since dawn,
And twenty bitter rogues we've found, no less!
They crouched behind the tall grey stones, or lay
Prone in the furze, or knelt at Calvaries!
Two women remain—

[He stares at **YVETTE** and **SÉRAPHINE**.

SÉRAPHINE
O Saint Thégonnec!
Saint Guirec! Saint Servan!

YVETTE
O Our Lady!

[Enter **THE ABBÉ**.

THE ABBÉ
De Vardes, your precious peasants—

[He sees **YVETTE**.

Who is here?
The De Méricourt, the mænad, I swear!
Who wounded De Vardes!

YVETTE
Oh!—

MME. DE VAUCOURT
The Egyptian!

SÉRAPHINE
Monseigneur, monseigneur, she's none of mine!

MLLE. DE CHÂTEAU-GUI
The poor girl!

SÉRAPHINE
Ah, mademoiselle, it is
The innocentest creature!

THE ABBÉ [Touches **YVETTE** upon the cheek]
Good-morning,
My dear!

COUNT LOUIS
Hm—m—m!—pretty!

THE VIDAME
Certainly the gallows
Should be thirty feet high.

COUNT LOUIS
Hm—m—m! Something less,
Monsieur le Vidame!

LALAIN
Diable!

DE VARDES [To the **SERGEANT**]
Where are your captives?

THE SERGEANT
My Colonel,
I have them safely here! Ha! you within!

[Enter from the hall of the château **SOLDIERS** and **HUNTSMEN** with **PEASANTS**, **MEN** and **WOMEN**; some sullenly submissive, others struggling against their bonds. They crowd the terrace before the great doors. The **GUESTS** of **DE VARDES** to the right and left upon the terrace, the stairs, and in the garden.

[**YVETTE** and **SÉRAPHINE** beside the statue; **LALAIN** near them; **DE VARDES** with his hand upon the great chair.

MME. DE VAUCOURT
Oh, the brigands!

COUNT LOUIS [Rubbing his hands]
Here, Sergeant, range them here,
Upon the terrace! And take the great chair,
De Vardes! Ma foi! We will teach them, the rogues!
Monsieur l'Anglais, have you peasants at home
Plague you at times?—Word of a gentleman!
It seems like old days and Henri again!

[The **SOLDIERS** thrust their prisoners forward with the butts of their muskets.

A MAN
Monseigneur!

ANOTHER
Monseigneur!

A WOMAN
Madame la Marquise!
My father was your father's foster brother!

THE MARQUISE
Is that a reason you should burn châteaux?

A YOUNG WOMAN
Where's Yvette Charruel?

YVETTE
Here, Angélique!

SÉRAPHINE [Aside to **ANGÉLIQUE**]
Of course! Betray the girl! I knew you would.

AN OLD WOMAN
Yvette said God would have mercy! I faint—

DE VARDES [To **GRÉGOIRE**]
Give her wine!

A PEASANT
See! There is Rémond Lalain!

LALAIN
Patience, compatriot! Thursday I speak
In the Jacobins!

ANGÉLIQUE
Ah, monseigneur!
Ah, monseigneur, there's she who led us here!
There's she who said the shadow of Morbec
Blackened the land as sin blackens the soul!

THE GUESTS
Ah!—

ANGÉLIQUE
That same Yvette, who said, monseigneur,
That delving the earth, the peasants of France
In a long age had delved up a thought!

The Guests
Ah!—

ANGÉLIQUE
She said that we were never born to starve!
She said the seigneur's dues were all infâme!

THE GUESTS
Ah!—

THE VIDAME
Burn the witch!

DE VARDES
Have you done?

ANGÉLIQUE
Monseigneur,
She said the forest deer, the hare, the birds,
Were just as much the peasant's as the lord's!

THE ENGLISHMAN
What? What?

ANGÉLIQUE
She said the saints they wished no tithes!

THE ABBÉ
I give her up!

ANGÉLIQUE
Monseigneur, monseigneur,
She said that all our hope was the tricolour!

DE BUC
O lilies of Bourbon!

SÉRAPHINE [To **ANGÉLIQUE**]
Thou little beast!

ANGÉLIQUE [Shrilly]
Yvette said bitter hunger, cold, and want
Came with noblesse and with noblesse would go!
Yvette said the Queen was an Austrian!
Yvette said the King was a fainéant!
Yvette said the princes were traitors!
Yvette said the armies would turn to us!
Yvette heard the drums of the Republic!

THE GUESTS
Out!

COUNT LOUIS
Enough!

SÉRAPHINE
Thou hellicat!

A PEASANT
Monseigneur!
Saint Yves le Véridique knows it is truth!
She ever rings the tocsin in our hearts!

ANOTHER
Yvette Charruel!

A WOMAN
She led us here!

Another Woman
Yvette!
Yvette Charruel!

ANGÉLIQUE
Yvette?—

[Several of the **WOMEN** laugh.

DE VARDES
Why, you are all cowards!

SÉRAPHINE
So they are, monseigneur, so they are!

DE VARDES [To the **PEASANTS**]
Who speaks for you?

[A silence.

THE PEASANTS
Monseigneur—monseigneur—

[They break off. **DE VARDES** stands waiting for them to speak, his hand upon the chair.

AN OLD WOMAN
Yvette—

AN OLD MAN
Yvette—

THE PEASANTS
Monseigneur—

[They break off. They make a sighing sound. The **OLD WOMAN** begins to say her beads.

YVETTE
Monseigneur,
They are so hungry! Monseigneur, 'tis said
You are a soldier and have been to war!
Oh, to us all there comes one battle-field
When we must look into a conqueror's eyes!
Think then upon that last dark plain and show
Mercy to us who in the shadow stand!
We are your enemies!

DE BUC

Faith of an officer!
De Vardes—

YVETTE
The children are crying at home,
Monseigneur!

A WOMAN
O Sainte Vierge, have pity!

YVETTE
With bowed heads the old men wait!

A WOMAN
Oh, my father!

YVETTE
The young men hear the ravens crying!

THE PEASANTS
Aie!—

YVETTE
The nets are dry, the red sails laid away,
And all the boats lie idle by the shore.

A FISHERMAN
Star of the Sea! Pray for poor fisherfolk!

A PEASANT
I left my sickle in the standing corn.

YVETTE
The wheat must fall, the flax be gathered soon,
Or else we'll sing no songs in Morbihan!

THE PEASANTS
Aie! The songs of the diskanerien!

YVETTE
The hearths are cold and the wheels turn not,
And Hunger sits on every doorstep!

THE PEASANTS
Aie!—

YVETTE
To-morrow is the Pardon of the Birds.

The birds go free—the birds go free, monseigneur!

DE BUC
And so I swear should you!

THE PEASANTS
The birds go free!

A WOMAN
My little bird at home!

THE MARQUISE
Give her, monsieur,
Another fan to break!

YVETTE
Not one of yours,
Madame la Marquise!

DE VARDES [To the **SERGEANT**]
Give them liberty.

THE SERGEANT
My Colonel?

DE VARDES
Cut their bonds; set them free!
Make way for them there!
[To **THE PEASANTS**]
Peasants of Morbec!
Last night you rose against your lord and strove
To burn his house, to slay his guest and him.
How shall he speak to you to-day? Poor fools!
Distraught and blind you struck ere that you looked,
And struck at one who fain would be your friend,
Who has his vision of a seigneur's right!
These are the towers of Morbec, but I
Am not Baron Henri, blind that ye are!
I am Baron René, remember my name.
Bread you shall have, I will think of your wrongs.
No foe am I! There are the open doors.
Back to the village go! but look you well.
Mistake no more, it will be dangerous!
Creep not this way again in the dark night,
Or you may meet an ancient Lord of Morbec!
More loyal grow, cease all your traitorous talk,
Raise not Rebellion's head or it will find
A soldier of the King with armèd heel!

Mistake no more! This once I pardon you.
Begone! The fields await you and the wind
Sits fair for Quiberon! Begone.
[To **YVETTE** and **SÉRAPHINE**]
Stay!

[**THE PEASANTS** press in confusion toward the doors of the château.

THE PEASANTS
Live Baron René!

LALAIN
O Breton fools!—Yvette!

[**YVETTE** does not answer. She looks at **DE VARDES**.

THE MARQUISE [With strained laughter]
High justice at Morbec!

THE VIDAME
Mille diables!
The wretches all go free!

COUNT LOUIS
Is this Morbec?
Mort de ma vie! What is it that you do,
Monsieur le Baron de Morbec?

DE VARDES
My pleasure,
Monsieur le Comte de Château-Gui, upon
My peasants of Morbec!

CURTAIN

ACT II

The garden of the Convent of the Visitation at Nantes. Long lines of fruit trees which appear to sleep in the sunshine. In the middle of the garden a stone fountain, where rises and falls a little jet of water. To the left the white buildings of the convent; in the background, between the convent and the street, a high garden wall, the tops of trees, and the roof and spire of a church. There is a barred door in the wall. The doors and windows of the convent parlour giving upon the garden are open. It is the summer of 1792.

A **NUN** appears for a moment at the door of the convent, then vanishes, and **DE VARDES** and **YVETTE** enter the garden.

DE VARDES
What hast thou learned to-day?

YVETTE
In history:
The battles of Rossbach and of Minden!
The Peace of Paris—

DE VARDES
Indeed!

YVETTE
Philosophy:
Man is born free—but who will break his chains?

DE VARDES
It is a question truly!

YVETTE
Theology:
God is the father of us all—and yet
I think I know how feels an orphan child!

DE VARDES
Defeat of France, Rousseau, and Modern Doubt!
And hast thou learnt all this in convent walls?

YVETTE
No!

DE VARDES
They are good to thee, the Sisters all?

YVETTE
Monseigneur, yes!

DE VARDES
When I did place thee here
After that day thou didst not burn Morbec!
I gave the Reverend Mother straitest charge,—
This convent oweth much to the De Vardes.
They have enriched it oft, and it in turn
Refuge hath given unto noble dames.
Oft did she sit beside the fountain there,
That Duchess Jeanne whose look thou wearest now!

YVETTE

Oh!—

DE VARDES
How mournfully thou sighest! Yet
How glorious are thine eyes this lovely day!
Thou'rt well, and thou art happy, art thou not?

YVETTE
There is no hunger here, no cold, no care!
I ever wished to learn and here I learn,
Here where the Duchess Jeanne did sit forlorn,—
And then I pray within the chapel there,
And then I count the stars as they are lit,—
And then I think of all the lights of Nantes!

DE VARDES
It hath been many days I've been away,
To Morbec and to Vannes and to Vitré.

YVETTE
I thought that thou wouldst never come again!

DE VARDES
Didst think the night had ceased to long for day?
Didst think the tide no more obeyed the moon?
The reed no longer bowed unto the wind?

YVETTE
Ah, do not jest!—There's blood upon thy coat!

DE VARDES
'Tis nothing!—We have had hard words to-day,
My men and I!

[He gazes around at the quiet garden.

O holy peace! O balm!
O green and sunny quietude! Outside
There's tumult, heat, confusion, enmity!
Here is a haven, here 'tis blissful sweet!

[They sit upon the marge of the fountain.

All is dismay and doubt in France to-day.
With troubled eyes men question destiny!
Outside I front the storm as best I may,
But here is anchorage profound and fair—
There fruit trees drifting bloom, this fountain marge!

YVETTE
I better love the wild and desolate shore!

DE VARDES
What is that ribbon closed within thy hand?

[**YVETTE** opens her hand and shows a ribbon cockade.

The tricolour!

YVETTE
Wilt thou not wear it?

DE VARDES
No!

YVETTE
It was my favour—Fare you well, monsieur!

DE VARDES
I might not wear that ribbon, no, not if
It were thy favour truly, Vivien!
Ah, when will cease this discord of our minds?
Wilt thou forever be a Jacobin?

[A distant bugle, followed by a roll of drums and martial music.

YVETTE
Aux armes, Citoyens!
Formez vos bataillons!

DE VARDES
Where learned'st thou the Marseillaise?

YVETTE
'Tis in the air! Oh, on these moonlight nights
I dream of France and how he spoke to me
Of all the wrongs of France we should redress!

DE VARDES
Who spoke to thee?

YVETTE
Rémond Lalain.

DE VARDES
Rémond Lalain was once my closest friend.

He travels now a dark and winding way!

YVETTE
Where is she now, that lady bright and fair
Who's named La Belle Marquise in Morbihan?

DE VARDES
She is in Nantes.

YVETTE
Ah!—Is she not fair?

DE VARDES
Most fair.

YVETTE
And nobly born?

DE VARDES
And nobly born.

YVETTE
Alas!

[Enter **SISTER BENEDICTA**.

SISTER BENEDICTA
Monsieur le Baron de Morbec,—
A courier, in haste, foam-flecked and spent,
Demands to speak with you.

DE VARDES
What tidings now?
Ill news like ravens to a cumbered field!
I come, my Sister!
[To **YVETTE**]
I'll return.

[Exeunt **DE VARDES** and **SISTER BENEDICTA**.

YVETTE
Alas!
She is in Nantes! He sees her every day.
What is this pain that's tearing at my heart?

[Laughing voices of young **GIRLS**. Enter from the convent **SISTER FIDELIS** and **SISTER SIMPLICIA** with a cluster of young **GIRLS**, pupils of the nuns or refugees from Royalist families. They seat themselves upon the wide steps of the fountain.

[**YVETTE** leans against the basin and plays in the water with her hand.

A YOUNG GIRL [To **YVETTE**]
We're telling stories!

ANOTHER
Finish thine, Louise!

LOUISE
'Tis told. The beau prince wed the belle princesse,
And they lived happily ever after!

A YOUNG GIRL
Whose turn now?

ANOTHER
Tell us a story, Yvette!

YVETTE [Turning from the fountain]
Beneath the halfway tree,
'Tween Josselin and Pontivy,
Suddenly, out of the dark,
I heard a grey wolf bark!
Hoée! Hoée! Hoée!
The snow was on the ground,
The shadows all around,
Laid a finger on my lip,
As I stood, hand on hip,
Listening the grey wolf bark.
Hoée! Hoée! Hoée!
Beneath the halfway tree,
'Tween Josselin and Pontivy!
A little child came by.
"Yvette, the wolf is nigh!
Yvette, take thou me up,
I've neither bite nor sup!"
Hoée! Hoée! Hoée!
The child came to my arm.
He was so fair and warm!
The child came to my arm,
I kept him safe from harm!
Hoée! Hoée! Hoée!
A light grew round his head,
I felt all cheered and fed.
"Yvette, have thou no fear!
Who giveth aid, to me is dear!"
Hoée! Hoée! Hoée!

The child no longer pressed,
White snow lay on my breast!
The grey wolf ran away,
Hoée! Hoée! Hoée!
There broke a splendid day,
Beneath the halfway tree,
'Tween Josselin and Pontivy!

SISTER FIDELIS
A miracle?

YVETTE
I do not know.

A YOUNG GIRL
I liked best
The beau prince and the belle princesse.

ANOTHER GIRL
Oh,
Thou'rt an Aristocrat!

[The young **GIRLS** return to their embroidery. **YVETTE** plays in the water of the fountain with her hand.

YVETTE
Gold fish, gold fish,
How are the fish of Quiberon?

A YOUNG GIRL
Were I
A fairy prince, then my princess should be
Madame la Marquise de Blanchefôret!

ANOTHER
If I
Were a princess, I would have for my prince
Monsieur le Baron de Morbec.

[**YVETTE** turns from the fountain.

A THIRD GIRL
They say
That in all France there's none more brave than he!
And far and near she's called La Belle Marquise!
A little while and there'll a wedding be!

THE FIRST
But then, the poor Yvette! He is, you know,

Her prince!

[They laugh.

YVETTE
Oh, mockery!

SISTER FIDELIS
Hush, children, hush!
Monsieur le Baron is her benefactor!

SISTER SIMPLICIA
He plucked her from the dreadful world outside!

SISTER FIDELIS
He placed her here beneath Our Lady's care.

SISTER SIMPLICIA
In everything he is her truest friend!

SISTER FIDELIS
But for his condescension, ah, who knows
What in these fearful days might be her lot!
Here in this fold she's safe.

YVETTE [Aside]
Alas! alas!
A Young Girl
Oh, she is fairer than the fairy queen!
Clarice de Miramand and Blanchefôret!

YVETTE [Aside]
Is she so fair? Is she so fair indeed?
I broke her fan—now she will break my heart!

A YOUNG GIRL
He is a knight like Lancelot!

YVETTE
Oh me!
She is the Queen, she is that Guinevere!

[Distant music. The noise of footsteps and voices in the street beyond the wall.

A YOUNG GIRL
Oh, outside the wall what is there passing?

SISTER FIDELIS [Severely]

We have nothing to do with outside the wall.

A YOUNG GIRL [Indicating the door in the wall]
Might we open the door a little way?

SISTER FIDELIS
The blessed saints forbid!

[From the street are heard the drums and fifes of passing National **TROOPS**. The bayonets of the **SOLDIERS** are visible above the wall.

VOICES [In the street]
Allons, enfants de la patrie,
Le jour de gloire est arrivé!

A YOUNG GIRL
Oh, soldiers!

ANOTHER
Were the wall only down!

[The circle about the fountain breaks. The young **GIRLS** walk up and down beneath the trees. The **SISTERS** watch them from a garden bench. The music dies away. **YVETTE** sits upon the stone marge of the fountain.

YVETTE
What is this pain that's tearing at my heart?
What matters it to me whom he doth love?
And what concern of mine that she is fair?
I would she were not so!—Oh, misery!
She is in Nantes, she is La Belle Marquise!
I would that she were dead!

[The chapel bell rings.

O Seigneur Dieu!
Her death! I do not wish her death! Not I!
O Our Lady! let not ill thoughts possess me!
I would I were at Morbec this still eve,
Herding the cows amid the golden broom,
Above a sea of glass without a wind,
As stagnant calm as is this prisoned water!
I would gather the musk rose in the lane,
I would tread the wet sand and count the ships,
My brow would not burn, my heart would not ache,
No tears from my eyes would I wipe away!
Why should they not fall like the winter rain?
I am the herd girl here as at Morbec,

And she's a great lady, loved for herself!
O love! is it love that stifles me so?
O love! is it love that makes me weep?
I thought that love was all splendour and light,
The bow in the sky, the bird at its height,
The glory and state of an angel bright!
What is this pain that burdens all my heart?

[She bows her head upon her knees. The hum of the street deepens to a continuous and sinister sound. In the distance a roll of drums.

[**YVETTE** raises her head.

I sit by this fountain, he'll not return!
He cares not for me,—he's the Sieur de Morbec,
And I a herd girl wandering through his fields!
Mother, my mother, did you sit and wait,
By the wild sea rim on a glowing eve,
Mid the brown seaweed on the shining sands?
Your heart did it beat, and your senses swim?—
But your lover, the fisher, he came, he came!

[The **VOICE** of the street deepens.

I will not have this pain! I'll tear it out!

[Her hand touches the purple mark on her throat.

Ha! how burns this hateful mark to-day!

[There comes from the church towers of Nantes a sudden and violent crash of bells.

SISTER FIDELIS [Rising]
The tocsin!

THE YOUNG GIRLS [They flutter forward to the fountain]
The tocsin! Oh, the tocsin!
Like a hive of bees hums the street without!

YVETTE
Oh, all ye iron bells! ring on! ring on!

[Enter **MLLE. DE CHÂTEAU-GUI** and SISTER BENEDICTA.

THE YOUNG GIRLS
Here is Mademoiselle de Château-Gui!
She'll tell us why the bells are ringing!

MLLE. DE CHÂTEAU-GUI
O Ciel!
Would you believe it? O blessed saints above!
The country is in danger!

A YOUNG GIRL
Oh! we thought
You brought us news!

MLLE. DE CHÂTEAU-GUI [Joyously]
Do you not hear the bells?
Oh, such a day outside! It is proclaimed!
La patrie est en danger!

[Distant trumpets.

Well you may wail,
You brazen trumpets of the Revolution!
The Duke of Brunswick he is marching now,
And with him all our nobles back from Coblentz!
O bliss! La patrie est en danger!

SISTER FIDELIS
Oh, hush!
The very walls have ears!

MLLE. DE CHÂTEAU-GUI
My father says
The King shall have his own again, and all
Will go as merry as a wedding bell!
La patrie est en danger!

[Enter **COUNT LOUIS**, **MELIPARS DE L'ORIENT**, and the **ABBÉ DE BARBASAN**.

Oh, here are
My father and Monsieur de L'Orient!

DE L'ORIENT
So sweet the flowers here—

COUNT LOUIS [To the young **GIRLS**]
Mesdemoiselles,
One garden of rosebuds time hath not touched!
[To the **SISTERS**]
In your prayers, my Sisters, name Château-Gui!

[The young **GIRLS** curtesy, then exeunt between the trees. **YVETTE** remains beside the fountain. **COUNT LOUIS** looks at her through his glass.

Ha!

DE L'ORIENT
The herd girl of Morbec!

COUNT LOUIS
I have eyes,
De L'Orient!

THE ABBÉ
Hm!—Fair child!

YVETTE [Coldly]
Citoyen!

MLLE. DE CHÂTEAU-GUI
Monsieur de L'Orient, you promised me
My father should not walk abroad to-day!

DE L'ORIENT
What could I do? He is so young and rash!

COUNT LOUIS [Taking snuff]
'Tis true that Nantes is dangerous to-day
To all save those wild beasts the sans-culottes!
But that's no reason I should stay at home.
Where is De Vardes? His man said he was here.
It is his wont, pardieu!

SISTER FIDELIS
Monsieur le Comte,
Monsieur the Baron of Morbec did come
To see that all was well with this our charge—
A peasant girl, monsieur, whom he did save
From cold and hunger and ill company.
But now she prospers and we think that he
Will come no more.

YVETTE
Jesu Maria!

COUNT LOUIS [With satisfaction]
Ma foi!
He is a soldier is De Vardes! He camps
One day beside the hedgerow in the field!
The next he's for some royal mount of love,
High as the snow and splendid in the sun!

Since he's not here I know where else he is!

DE L'ORIENT [Sings]
Mignonne, Mignonne!
Kiss me, rose of to-day!

YVETTE
O heart! O world! O hedgerow in the field!

COUNT LOUIS
Well, well, her mother was as fair as she!
Clarice de Miramand, long-dead Clarice!
Her hair was golden too.—Old times, old times!
And now it is De Vardes and the Marquise!

[**COUNT LOUIS, MLLE. DE CHÂTEAU-GUI**, and **DE L'ORIENT** walk up and down beneath the trees. **DE L'ORIENT** sings.

DE L'ORIENT
Mignonne, Mignonne!
The red rose fades away!
Mignonne, Mignonne!
The white rose will not stay!

THE ABBÉ
My dear, that is a pretty wrist of thine!

YVETTE
Citoyen!

THE ABBÉ
Hast said thy rosary to-day?

YVETTE
Citoyen!

THE ABBÉ
A melting eye!

YVETTE
Citoyen!

THE ABBÉ
Dame! She is only good to burn châteaux!

[He joins **COUNT LOUIS**, etc. They walk and talk beneath the trees.

YVETTE

The high of heart bide no man's scorning! I
Will break these bonds! I will be free! I will!
O royal mount of love, snow-high, sun-kissed,
Kissed by the sun which once did shine on me!
If I am of the fields—

[Her hand touches the mark upon her throat. She laughs.

O hated flower,
Which grew beneath no hedgerow on this earth!
Teach me, thou poison blossom, pride of heart!
Where is that Duchess Jeanne whom I am like?
They say for love her heart did rive in twain,
But now she smiles beside a shadowy stream
In some far land where none do die of love!
And where is he, Jehan the fisherman,
Who loved Yvonne, who met the sea and died?
They died for love who should have lived for hate!
I'll live—

[Enter **DE VARDES**. **COUNT LOUIS**, etc., come forward.

Oh, here's the soldier! Now we'll know
How blow the winds around the camp of love!

COUNT LOUIS
What is it, René de Vardes? What is it, man?

DE VARDES
The King hath left the Tuileries! The mob
Forced the château and put his life in danger.
The Swiss are murdered, cut down to a man!
The Grenadiers joined with the Marseillaise!
De Maillé writes—the courier's just arrived—
All is distraction, danger, and despair!

SISTER FIDELIS
Alas!

MLLE. DE CHÂTEAU-GUI
O Ciel!

THE ABBÉ
The soldiers in revolt.

DE L'ORIENT
The Swiss all murdered—the stanch Swiss!

SISTER SIMPLICIA
Alas!

COUNT LOUIS
The King hath left the Tuileries!

DE VARDES
To-night
I ride to Paris.

YVETTE
O God!

THE ABBÉ
To Paris!
As well say that you ride to death, De Vardes!

COUNT LOUIS
Ah, were I young again, I'd ride with you!

SISTER FIDELIS
Alas, they say it is a fearful place!

SISTER SIMPLICIA
It is so safe in Nantes!

DE VARDES
Ah, my Sister,
Because it is so safe in Nantes I go!
Once I did love this people; once I thought
Beyond this Revolution lay the morn,
The dewy morn of a most noble day!
It may be so; I know not; but I am
A soldier of the King. Needs must I go,
My bugles call; I'm breaking camp. Farewell!

SISTER FIDELIS
You will return.

DE VARDES
If I'm in life I will!

YVETTE
O Our Lady! O Our Lady!

[The noise in the street increases. The tocsin rings. The sky begins to darken before an approaching storm.

COUNT LOUIS
Ring on!
Ye bells! ring on to the deaf sky! O France,
Of old thou wast a pleasant land and free,
In palace and in field a courteous place!
Now thou art desolate! Come, Austria, come!
Come, D'Artois, come, Brunswick, and come, Provence!
Rend the tricolour from the breast of France
And plant the fleur-de-lis where stood the Jacobins!

VOICES [From the street]
Quoi! ces cohortes étrangères
Feraient la loi dans nos foyers!

MLLE. DE CHÂTEAU-GUI
Hast said farewell to the Marquise?

DE VARDES
Not yet,
As far as Vannes I ride beside her coach.

YVETTE
Oh!—

MLLE. DE CHÂTEAU-GUI
Soon or late, she'll draw you back to Nantes!
Now will she not?

DE VARDES [Smiling]
Perhaps.

YVETTE
Jesu Maria!

SISTER FIDELIS
Monsieur, if you must go, oh, rest you sure
Jealously will we guard and spotless keep
The soul you stooped and drew from the foul mire!—
Yvette, come make your reverence to your lord!

YVETTE
I kiss your hand, monseigneur!

THE ABBÉ
There will be
A storm to-night!

COUNT LOUIS

Come, come, René de Vardes!
I'd see the courier who brought this news!

DE VARDES
I'll follow you, Monsieur le Comte!

[Exeunt **COUNT LOUIS**, his daughter, **DE L'ORIENT**,

THE ABBÉ, and the Sisters.

YVETTE
Wilt thou go?

DE VARDES
I must.

YVETTE
Why must thou go?
To-day the kingdom fell! Oh, in the dust
Of old things let it rest for evermore!
Take up the Revolution!

[Lightning.

Oh, see!
The flaming sword before the gates of Eden!
Thou'rt safe within the garden! Go not forth.
Go not to Paris! Stay in Nantes, ah, stay!
Wear the tricolour—

[Thunder.

Hark! It is the voice,
The menacing voice of the Republic!
It threatens thee, it threatens all who pass
That flaming sword, to lift the thing that was
And is not any more! Oh, let it lie!—
Thou'lt not to Paris?

DE VARDES
To-night, Citoyenne!
Ah, thou art skilful at betraying!

YVETTE
Quoi!

[Enter **SISTER BENEDICTA**.

SISTER BENEDICTA
Monsieur le Baron de Morbec, the page
Of Madame la Marquise de Blanchefôret
Attends—

YVETTE
Name of a name!

THE ABBÉ [Appearing in the door behind **SISTER BENEDICTA**]
De Vardes, De Vardes!
You gather the furze while the red rose waits!

DE VARDES
At once, my Sister!
[To **YVETTE**]
Ah, not in anger,
Must thou and I part for this little while!
If I'm in life I will return, be sure,
To Nantes and all this garden loveliness,
Those fruit trees and this fountain!—Fare thee well.
The nuns will care for thee; I've ordered all.
Too fierce of aspect is the world without!
Here is fair peace, security, and calm;
Here thou art fenced from storm and violence.
Abide thou here until I come again!

[Lightning.

YVETTE
The flaming sword!

DE VARDES
Hearest thou not, Yvette,
How sings the lark in Paimpont Wood to-day?

YVETTE
I hear the dirge of the salt sea!

DE VARDES
And there,
Seest thou not through yonder trees the stone,
The Druid Stone where thou didst lie in sleep?

YVETTE
I see a broken fan!

DE VARDES
Abide thou here

And dream of Paimpont Wood until I come.
I too will dream, I too will dream, Yvette!

YVETTE
Is not Clarice a lovely name?

DE VARDES
Why, yes,
A very lovely name.—Farewell, farewell!
I'll see thy face, be sure, this very night,
Upon the road before me as I ride.

YVETTE
Oh, fare you well beneath the silver moon
As slow you ride beside a lady's coach,
Discoursing of the dazzling, snowy heights!
I kiss your hand, monseigneur! Fare you well!

[**THE ABBÉ**'s voice is heard from the doorway.

THE ABBÉ
De Vardes! De Vardes!

DE VARDES
I come!

THE ABBÉ
The rose awaits!—

YVETTE
It is too much!

DE VARDES
Farewell, thou spirit of Paimpont!

[Distant music.

YVETTE
Ah, ah! 'tis worth all else—the Marseillaise!

DE VARDES
My Duchess Jeanne—

YVETTE
She is dead: cold and dead!
Aux armes, Citoyens!
Formez vos bataillons!

DE VARDES
Perverse and strange!

YVETTE
I'll to my beads. Adieu!
Over Ys, the sunken town,
When thou sailest look not down,
Mariner, mariner!

DE VARDES
What wine hast thou drunken?

YVETTE
An old wine—
For there dwells a fairy there
Will drag thee down by the long hair,
Mariner, mariner!

DE VARDES
Oh, thou art too wilful!

THE ABBÉ
De Vardes! De Vardes!

YVETTE [To the fish in the fountain]
Gold fish, gold fish, how are the fish of Quiberon?

DE VARDES
Thou sullen witch, adieu!

[Exit **DE VARDES**.

YVETTE
Monseigneur! ah!
He's gone! He's gone to meet the fairy queen!
He's for the roses and the dazzling peaks!
The seaweed and the furze he's left behind!
He's left the storm, he's left the storm and me!

[The convent bell rings.

Toll, toll! as though thou'd toll my soul away!
Thou canst not toll him back! Oh, woe is me!

[The **NUNS** sing in the chapel.

VOICES
O salutaris Hostia!

Quae coeli pandis ostium:
Bella premunt hostilia,
Da robur fer auxilium!

[Above the wall where it is shadowed by a fruit tree, appear the head and shoulders of **LALAIN**. He draws himself up to the coping, watches **YVETTE** for a moment, then swings himself down to the garden. He has a rose in his hand.

YVETTE
Where is the sunshine gone? Where is the gold?
It was a lovely day! 'Tis cold and dead;
No light, no warmth, no cheer!—Oh, presently
Those two will take the summer road to Vannes!
Ha! does he think that I will meekly stay
Within this convent close, will kneel and pray,
Day in, day out, for all true lovers' weal?
What is there now to do?—O Jealousy!
I dream of Paimpont Wood in June! I'll dream
Of sunlit peaks, of roses named Clarice;
I'll dream of furze that's set about with thorns
And clings unto the common earth which bore it!

[A roll of thunder.

On, on! It suits my mood, the crashing sound!—
Jehan the fisherman! rise from the sea,
Lay thy cold hand upon the heart of her
Who's not thy child, and teach her how to hate!
Yvonne who parted from the earth one night,
Come through the storm that darkens overhead
And teach thy daughter how to hate! Thou too,
Thou other one, thou seigneur high and grand
Whose signet burns upon my aching throat,
Whose nature stirs within me suddenly,
Arise from hell and teach me how to hate!

[Thunder.

VOICES FROM THE CHAPEL
Tantum ergo sacramentum
Veneremur cernui—

YVETTE
O Our Lady! O Our Lady! O Our Lady!

[**LALAIN** throws the rose. It falls beside **YVETTE**.

Oh!—

[She raises the flower to her lips. **LALAIN** comes forward.

Thou! I thought it was—I thought it was.
Go! No rose of thine would I have kissed,
Rémond Lalain!

[With a wild petulance she throws down the flower and treads upon it.

LALAIN
Now for that deed of thine
I will not spare him when the day is mine!

YVETTE
Of whom speakest thou?

LALAIN
The Citoyen Vardes.

YVETTE
Let him be!

LALAIN
The Citoyenne Blanchefôret.

YVETTE
Again!

LALAIN
'Tis said the two will shortly wed—
A fitting match!—She's fair and nobly born.
Thou mightst have seen, thou mightst have seen last night,
Walking by moonlight beside the Loire,
A lady the fairest and a great lord!

YVETTE
Say'st thou?

LALAIN
Beneath the trees, beside the flood,
Toying and whispering, the sword and fan!

YVETTE
Out and alas! Begone, thou torturer!

LALAIN
Oh, those old days when by the shore we walked
While sank the sun beneath the emerald waves,

And wild sea birds flashed all their silver wings,
And long we talked of France and liberty!
How thou art tamed, Yvette, Yvette Charruel!
Thou carest not now for France and liberty!

YVETTE
It is not true! Thou knowest that I care!

LALAIN
This sultry night I speak to patriot hearts
Of War, Dumouriez, Brunswick, Capet!
All Nantes will throng to hear me where I stand,
In the Church of Saint Jean, who's now become,
From crypt to spire, one mighty Jacobin!
High in the gilt tribune beneath the roof,
The starry roof where the archangels live!
Faces me Michael with his flaming sword,
And Raphael watches me with widened eyes,
And Gabriel frowns between his splendid wings
Because there's no more incense! When I speak,
The painted walls all vanish like a mist!
On distant plains the drum begins to beat,
The great dome lifts—above the angel heads
I see the stars—

YVETTE
There are no stars to-night!

LALAIN
There are! There are! Eternally they shine
Beyond this din, beyond these sulphurous clouds!
And there's a stairway, red and white and blue,
By which to climb to some most famous star
Of glory and of love! Yvette! Yvette!
Climb thou with me unto that golden star!

YVETTE
Rémond Lalain—

LALAIN
Come thou with me, Yvette!
Come thou with me from out this sluggish place!
Come thou with me into the furious storm!
What dost thou here, thou spirit of the wind,
Restless, with deep eyes and with parted lips?
Thou knowest thou hast naught to do with holy things.
Tear off that white headdress! Red is thy colour!

YVETTE
Ay, red is my colour!

LALAIN
Last night, the while
I spake of War and all the place was still,
A sudden vision blazed above the lights—
I saw thee dance the Carmagnole!

YVETTE
Now, now!
What whispers he to her upon the road?

LALAIN
To-night—ah, should I raise my eyes to-night
And see thee smiling there, Yvette, Yvette!
Beside thy sisters in the galleries!
Upon thy twilight hair the bonnet-rouge,
At thy small waist a pistol and a dirk—
Only the Revolution in thy soul
And in thy heart my name, my name, Yvette!

[Thunder.

It thunders now, but 'twill be clear to-night.
The moon will shine, the roads will all be white.

YVETTE
The roads will all be white, the moon will shine,
The poplars quiver and the eglantine,
The broom and honeysuckle will be sweet,
Upon the road to Vannes—

[Lightning and thunder.

[**LALAIN** walks to the door in the wall, tries it, then with a stone from the ground beats back the rusty bolt.

LALAIN
An easy door!

YVETTE
The moon will shine—

LALAIN
I'll go this way, ma foi!
Not by the wall!

YVETTE
The silver poplars sway!

LALAIN
René de Vardes, once I did call thee friend
And took a deal of pride in that possession!
How runs the world away! 'Twas long ago!

YVETTE
Ah, ah, that fearful dream I had last night!
And while I dreamed they walked beside the Loire!

LALAIN
This night he rides away. Didst know?

YVETTE
I knew!

LALAIN
He's said farewell to thee, but not to her!

YVETTE
Wilt thou begone!

LALAIN
Ay, through this door, Yvette!
'Tis easy, as thou seest. And ah, to-night—
The storm o'er past and shining bright the moon
And the cold nuns all telling o'er their beads,
How simple 'twere—O priceless liberty!
Thou wouldst not be the only one, I trow,
Who may not walk beside the silver Loire!

YVETTE
Name of a name!

LALAIN
Adieu, adieu! To-night
I'll see thee sitting in the galleries—

[Exit **LALAIN**.

YVETTE
Ah, how the thunder shakes the air!

[She moves to the door in the wall and replaces the bolt, then returns to the fountain.

'Tis so!

He is her lover! Oh, he loves her true!—
What will they say and whisper all the night
Through light and shadow on the road to Vannes?
Despair!—But I'll not stay within these walls!

[Knocking at the door in the wall.

[**YVETTE** crosses the stage to the door.

Who is there?

SÉRAPHINE [Within]
Yvette! Yvette!

YVETTE
Séraphine!

SÉRAPHINE [Within]
And Nanon too!

YVETTE
The deputy's sister!

NANON
Let us in!

YVETTE
I dare not.

SÉRAPHINE
What!

YVETTE
Wait: I dare!

[She draws the bolts. The door opens. Enter **SÉRAPHINE** and **NANON**. The former is dressed in complete carmagnole: short skirt, rolled-up sleeves, sash of tricolour, and a bonnet-rouge. Pistols at her belt. **NANON** is more soberly attired but wears the bonnet-rouge. The door closes behind them.

Séraphine!

SÉRAPHINE
Chérie!

YVETTE
Nanon!

NANON

Dear Yvette!

YVETTE
How gay you are! What of the Revolution?

SÉRAPHINE
It goes.

NANON
It goes well.

SÉRAPHINE
We have a new song!
Faith! 'Tis a greater song than Ça Ira!

YVETTE [Sings]
Aux armes, Citoyens!
Formez vos bataillons!

SÉRAPHINE
That's it!

NANON [Looking about her]
So very triste it is in here!

SÉRAPHINE
So gay outside! All Nantes is dressed in red!
There's a procession, and then to-night
We sit in the galleries to hear Lalain!

[Distant music.

Hark to the fife! Formez vos bataillons!—
And your feet keep not time to the music!

YVETTE
But my heart, Séraphine, my heart keeps time.

SÉRAPHINE
Ho! Your heart is in barracks, says Céleste.

YVETTE
Céleste!

NANON
And Angélique.

YVETTE

Angélique!

SÉRAPHINE
Faith!
Angélique is in feather now you're gone!
Cries Vive la République! here in Nantes.
Rides on the cannon and handles a pike;
Thinks she's in Paris and plays Théroigne,
And high from the galleries applauds Lalain!

NANON
He thinks not of her; he thinks of Yvette!

YVETTE
I care not of whom he thinks!

SÉRAPHINE
On a fête day,
In a car triumphal see her appear!
Dressed like a goddess just down from the skies,
All crowned with green oak leaves, borne shoulder high—

YVETTE
Angélique!

SÉRAPHINE [Nodding]
Ah, you see you are not there!
But between you and me, red does not become her!

YVETTE
I should think not!—little blonde!

SÉRAPHINE
Ah, but red
Becomes you!

YVETTE
Yes!

SÉRAPHINE
Monseigneur's gone from Nantes.
Yes, faith! I saw him ride away—

YVETTE
He's gone!
Rememb'rest thou that lady fair and proud,
Madame la Marquise de Blanchefôret?

SÉRAPHINE
Ho!
[To **NANON**]
Rememb'rest thou the Citoyenne Blanchefôret?

NANON
The proud piece! We are mire beneath her feet!
Last eve her coach threw mud upon my gown!
Let her beware! One day she'll walk afoot.
Let her beware! And let him too beware
Who rode last eve beside her golden coach!

YVETTE
Ha, ha! ha, ha!

[Music and voices in the street. Impatient knocking at the door in the wall.

VOICES
Holà, Aristocrats!
Nanon! Séraphine!

NANON
Our friends await us.

SÉRAPHINE
We have business with the smith upon the quai,
Where by the old dovecot he fashions pikes!

VOICES
Allons, enfants de la patrie!

NANON
Come, come away! We'll leave the nun alone
To say her beads for black Aristocrats!
How triste to be for aye in prison here!

YVETTE [Angrily]
Prison! I am no prisoner, I!

NANON
Then come with us into the merry streets!

SÉRAPHINE
'Twill be a heavy storm—all are within.
How easy 'twere to slip away with us!

YVETTE
No, no!

VOICES
Citoyennes! Citoyennes!

NANON
Ma'm'selle!

YVETTE
Ma'm'selle!

NANON
Aristocrat!

YVETTE
Aristocrat!

SÉRAPHINE
Well—kept by an Aristocrat—

YVETTE
You lie.

SÉRAPHINE [Angrily]
Saint Yves! I lie! Do I? O Seigneur Dieu!
This is Yvette, the herd girl of Morbec!
This is Yvette, the daughter of Yvonne!
This is that same Yvette who swore one day
That rather would she meet the blight of hell
Than take one favour from a seigneur's hand!
Once you were hungry! Go you hungry now?
You went in rags. Where is your ragged gown?
Barefoot—what's that about that throat of thine?
I swear it is a jewel!—and we pine
For bread, we women of the Revolution!

[**YVETTE** unclasps the jewel from her neck and lets it fall.

I lie, do I? Diable! Just prove I lie!
This night we make a little noise in Nantes
Shall show Aristocrats who is in danger!
Lalain will speak and all the bells will ring,
And Angélique will deck herself in red!
Steal through yon door, be of us evermore!
I lie, do I? Then show me that I lie!

YVETTE
In Nantes where do you lodge?

SÉRAPHINE
With Angélique
Under the Lanterne, Sign of the Hour Glass.

VOICES
Nanon! Nanon! You are missing the sights!

[Distant music.

OTHER VOICES
Allons, enfants de la patrie,
Le jour de gloire est arrivé!

NANON
Come, come away!

[**SÉRAPHINE** unbars the door in the wall. It swings open.

SÉRAPHINE
Faith! One can see the Loire!
'Tis fine to walk beside it 'neath the moon!

YVETTE
Oh!—

VOICES
Tremblez, tyrans! et vous perfides,—

NANON
Away! Away!

YVETTE
I'll go—I'll go with you.
Ye fruit trees and thou fountain, fare ye well!

[Exeunt **YVETTE**, **SÉRAPHINE**, **NANON**. The door swings to. Lightning and thunder. **SISTER FIDELIS** appears in the convent door.

VOICES [Dying away]
Aux armes, Citoyens!
Formez vos bataillons!

CURTAIN

A square in Nantes. On the left the deep porch of a church with pillars. To the right and in the background, a perspective of streets with tall, many-windowed houses. Opposite the church a great plaster statue of Liberty. Over the church door is written in white lettering: "The Republic One and Indivisible. Liberty, Equality, Fraternity or Death. National Property." A distant view of the Loire. **MEN** and **WOMEN** in holiday garb, wearing liberty caps and great tricoloured cockades, cross and recross the square. Life, movement, colour. Red the dominant note. It is the year 1794.

Hoarse voices within. Hawkers of Revolutionary journals cross the square.

A HAWKER
Le Journal des Jacobins!

ANOTHER
Le Discours
De la Lanterne!

[Enter **GRÉGOIRE**.

A THIRD
L'Orateur du Peuple!

A FOURTH
Le père Duchesne! Le Père Duchesne!

GRÉGOIRE [Stopping him]
Here!—

[He buys a paper.

And what to-day says Père Duchesne?

THE HAWKER
He says
That Paris envies Nantes her Carrier!

GRÉGOIRE
Humph!

A HAWKER
La Bouche de Fer!

ANOTHER
Les Actes des Apôtres!

A CITIZEN
I'll buy the Actes.

ANOTHER

I'll buy the Bouche de Fer.

[Enter a **MAN** with a long brush and a pot of paste. He proceeds to cover the wooden base of the Statue of Liberty with placards.

THE CROWDS
The placards! The placards!

A BRETON SAILOR
I cannot read!

[He catches by the arm a man in a long cloak, with a broad hat pulled low over his face.

Prithee, Citizen, what says the placard?

THE MAN IN THE CROWD
It says Duport is dead; Biron is dead;
Barnave is dead.

THE CROWD
Ha, ha! Biron! Barnave!

A MAN
Through the little window they've looked at last!
À bas les Aristocrats! Vive la Guillotine!

ANOTHER
Ah, here in Nantes we drown them in the Loire!

THE CROWD
Vive Carrier! Vive Lambertye! Vive Lalain!

[The **MAN** with the brush affixes a second placard.

THE BRETON
And this, Citizen?

THE MAN IN THE CLOAK
D'Alleray is dead;
Bailly is dead; Du Barry is dead.

THE CROWD
Ha!

A WOMAN
Ho! ho! The courtesan, she'll kiss no more!

THE CROWD

She'll kiss no more!

[The **MAN** with the brush affixes the third placard.

THE BRETON
And this one, Citizen?

THE MAN IN THE CLOAK [Reads]
The Republic One and Indivisible.
It is Decreed
There is no God. To-day we worship Reason.

[The **CROWD** applauds.

A MAN
In a red mantle!

ANOTHER
That's the Paris Reason!
Our Reason wears blue.

A THIRD
And oak leaves in her hair.

THE BRETON
Is Reason truly a woman?

THE MAN IN THE CLOAK
God knows!

A MAN
Ha! he says God! God is a word forbid!

THE MAN IN THE CLOAK
Then Reason knows.

A MAN
That's better.

[Singing within. A band of **DANCERS**, **MEN** and **WOMEN**, whirl into the square.

THE CROWD
Carmagnole!

THE DANCERS
Dansons la Carmagnole!
Vive le son, vive le son!
Dansons la Carmagnole!

Vive le son du canon!

[The **CROWD** breaks and joins the **DANCERS**. They take hands and with uncouth and extravagant gestures circle once or twice around the statue, then with a long cry exeunt.

A WOMAN
The great procession forms upon the quai!

ANOTHER
It winds and winds about and comes this way!

[Exeunt **MEN** and **WOMEN**. **GRÉGOIRE** and the **MAN** in the cloak remain.

GRÉGOIRE
The priests are gone. It is Reason's fête day.

THE MAN IN THE CLOAK
Reason, being a woman, will have her way.

GRÉGOIRE
Still, Monsieur l'Abbé—

THE ABBÉ
I am known!

GRÉGOIRE
To serve
Monsieur, I had the honour at Morbec.

THE ABBÉ
Monsieur le Baron's seneschal, I think.

GRÉGOIRE
The same,—but I am gaoler now in Nantes.

THE ABBÉ
That night in June your musket would not fire!
Diable! I've played and lost! Well, fellow?

GRÉGOIRE
Hein?

THE ABBÉ
The wind blows cold in Nantes, and so I wear
This cloak! So long I've looked on fires of hell
I needs must have a hat to shade my eyes!—
But now I'll cock it in the face of all—
Cold, wind, darkness, devils, and Republic!

GRÉGOIRE
I think the citizen has lost his head.

THE ABBÉ
Ay, and my heart as well. Holà! what's that?

[A noise without. Clash of steel and excited voices.

[Enter **DE VARDES** and **FAUQUEMONT DE BUC** pursued by seven or eight red-capped **MEN** armed with pikes. **DE VARDES** and **DE BUC** use their swords.

THE RED CAPS
Aristocrats! Aristocrats!

DE VARDES [Thrusting]
Take that,
Republican!

DE BUC [Thrusting]
Out, canaille!

THE ABBÉ
Here's wine!
Have at you, brow-bound galley slaves!

DE VARDES [Over his shoulder]
Ha! De Barbasan!

[Wounds his adversary.

We're at our last château!

THE ABBÉ
I've shut Voltaire! Here goes the candle out!

[He throws his long cloak over the head of **ONE** of the red caps and makes at **ANOTHER** with his dagger.

DE VARDES
The window splinters!

[He sends the pike flying from a red cap's hand.

Take warning, sans-culottes!

THE ABBÉ
One, two, three!

DE BUC
My sword arm!

DE VARDES
Fight with your left.
I saw you do it at Nanci!

VOICES [Within]
Ah! ça ira, ça ira, ça ira!
Les Aristocrats à la Lanterne!

DE VARDES
O Richard, O mon Roi,
L'univers t'abandonne!

[A howl from the **MOB**.

THE MOB
Aristocrats!

GRÉGOIRE [From the statue]
Desperate!

[The **RED CAPS**, **DE VARDES**, **THE ABBÉ**, and **DE BUC** fight across the stage and exeunt.

[**GRÉGOIRE** follows them.

VOICES [Within]
Ça ira!

[Enter **WOMEN** and **CHILDREN** of the Revolution.

A WOMAN
Upon the church steps I will take my stand!

ANOTHER
I have brought my knitting.

A THIRD
And I.

A FOURTH
And I.

ALL [Singing]
We are the tricoteuses!
Dyed wool we knit while rumbles by the cart.
Knit! knit! all knitting in the sun.

We are the tricoteuses!
Red wool we knit while soul and body part.
Knit! knit! the knitting now is done!

[They seat themselves upon the church steps.

A CHILD
Maman! Maman! how many carts will pass?

A WOMAN
None, sweeting, none! It is a holiday.

[Enter **CÉLISTE**, **ANGÉLIQUE**, and **NANON**.

NANON
It was the very night of the great storm
From those dull convent walls she ran away!

CÉLISTE
Two years agone—

ANGÉLIQUE
Would she had stayed!

NANON
Ah, then,
You had been Goddess, Angélique!

ANGÉLIQUE
The witch!
With her dark skin and with her purple flower!
Let her beware! I know a thing or two!

CÉLISTE
I know who comes from Paris back to Nantes!
This morning on the quai I saw him!

NANON [Eagerly]
Is't
That ci-devant, that black Aristocrat,
De Vardes?

CÉLISTE
The man your brother loves? The same.

NANON
I spit upon his name!

CÉLISTE
Denounced!

NANON
The set of sun
Will see him so, or my name's not Nanon!

CÉLISTE
The Loire—the Loire will close above his head!

[Enter **SÉRAPHINE**.

SÉRAPHINE
Whose head?

NANON
The Citizen Vardes.

SÉRAPHINE
Monseigneur!
He's in the prison of La Force at Paris!—
One truly told me so—He's not in Nantes.

NANON
And if he were—

SÉRAPHINE [Stammering]
Why—why—

NANON
And if he were,
You would not give him up! I know you well!
I know you, Séraphine!

SÉRAPHINE
And if you do,
You know no ill of me, Citoyenne!

CÉLISTE
Yvette
Would not give him up either.

ANGÉLIQUE
No, i' faith!
I'll take my oath on that!

SÉRAPHINE
Your oath, lint-locks!

It's worth a deal, your oath! Your mind I know!
You would be Goddess, you and not Yvette!

ANGÉLIQUE
Let her beware!

SÉRAPHINE
Yvette! She's coming now!
Bright as the star that's highest in the night!
And all the men have turned astronomers!
Faith! 'tis easy work to worship Reason,
When Reason is a woman, and that fair!

ANGÉLIQUE
I've seen her gather seaweed on the shore!

SÉRAPHINE
And now she gathers hearts in her two hands.

ANGÉLIQUE
Oh! oh!

NANON
Would that my brother hated her!
Disdainful prude!

CÉLISTE
Oh, love may turn to hate.
She's Goddess now, but wait, but wait, but wait!

NANON
I join my brother at the Olive Tree.
Come, Angélique, Céleste!

[Exeunt **NANON**, **ANGÉLIQUE**, **CÉLISTE**.

SÉRAPHINE
Were't not too late,
I'd warn monseigneur just for old time's sake!
When all is said and done, old times are best;
He gave us back Lisette, he fed us all—
Eh! 'twere a pity. What now? Who's this?

[Enter hurriedly **THE MARQUISE**. She looks over her shoulder as if fearing pursuit, then, drawing her cloak and hood closely about her, attempts to cross the square unobserved.

[Enter a rabble of **MEN** and **WOMEN**.

THE MOB
Ah! ça ira, ça ira, ça ira!
Les Aristocrats à la Lanterne.
Ah! ça ira, ça ira, ça ira!
Les Aristocrats on les pendra!

A TRICOTEUSE
She hides
Her face.

ANOTHER
She draws her cloak about her!

THE FIRST
Ho!
Her hand is white and there's a jewel on't!

A MAN [Accosting **THE MARQUISE**]
Citoyenne!

THE MARQUISE
Citoyen—

THE MAN
Citoyenne, come!
Join our ronde patriotique, our carillon!

THE MARQUISE
Sainte Geneviève!

THE MAN
What?

A WOMAN [Her hand upon **THE MARQUISE**]
Where's your cockade?

ANOTHER WOMAN
Show!

THE MARQUISE
De grâce, Citoyennes!

THIRD WOMAN
The cloak! The cloak!

[They tear from **THE MARQUISE** her hood and cloak.

A CHILD

Oh, the pretty lady!

THE MARQUISE
I'll give you gold!
There, there!—My rings, my brooch—take all!
Ah! let me peaceably depart—

THE MOB
Ha! ha!
Aristocrat!

A WOMAN
It is the emigrée
Clarice-Marie Miramand Blanchefôret!
Are not her gold locks known in Brittany?

ANOTHER
She fled to England.

A THIRD
She returned.

THE MARQUISE
O death!
[To a **WOMAN**]
Citoyenne, your cockade! I'll wear it gladly,
Ay, o'er my heart I'll pin it—

[She takes the cockade from the **WOMAN** and with trembling fingers pins it to her gown.

THE WOMAN
Red cap as well—

THE MARQUISE
With pleasure, Citoyenne.

[She places the bonnet-rouge upon her head.

THE MOB
Ha, ha!

A MAN
Now cry
Vive la République!

THE MARQUISE
Vive la République!

THE MAN
Mort aux tyrans!

THE MARQUISE
Mort aux tyrans!

THE MAN
À bas
Les Aristocrats!

[Silence.

THE MOB
Ah—h—h!

THE MAN
Vive la Guillotine!

[Silence.

A WOMAN
Take that!

[She strikes at **THE MARQUISE**.

THE MOB
Down! Down!

[**THE MARQUISE** breaks through the ring of men and women and runs to **SÉRAPHINE**.

THE MARQUISE
I know your face!
You are a Morbec woman! Save me! Save!

SÉRAPHINE
Saint Servan! Saint Gildas! Saint Mériadek!—
Ay, madame, you should have stayed in England!

[Enter **DE VARDES**, torn and bleeding.

DE VARDES
De Buc taken and De Barbasan! Dieu!
The day's not old. I'll see them ere its close.
We'll meet, I think, at Carrier's judgment bar,
Then the dark river,—and then peace at last—

THE MARQUISE
À moi, Monsieur le Baron de Morbec!

DE VARDES
La belle Marquise!

[He forces his way to the side of **THE MARQUISE**.

SÉRAPHINE [From the church porch]
Saint Yves le Véridique!

THE MOB
Both! Both!

A TRICOTEUSE
To prison with them!

ANOTHER
To the Loire!
Ho! ho! Les Noces Républicaines!

[The **MOB** surges forward, but with his sword **DE VARDES** keeps a clear space about him and **THE MARQUISE**. They move slowly backward to the church steps, which they mount.

DE VARDES [To **THE MARQUISE**]
We'll smile and die!

THE MARQUISE
Together, yes!

THE MOB
Down! Down! Aristocrats!

[**DE VARDES** sends a knife whirling from the hand of a red cap.

DE VARDES
Follow! Follow!
[To **THE MARQUISE**]
I have been long in prison.

THE MARQUISE
In England I!—And there I pined for France—
This sunshine dazzles me—

DE VARDES
Clarice-Marie!

[Trumpets within.

SÉRAPHINE

Hark! Hark, Citoyens, to the trumpets blowing!

THE MOB
She comes! Nantes' goddess comes!

[Faces appear at the windows of the tall houses.

A TRICOTEUSE
The windows fill!

[The rolling of drums.

ANOTHER TRICOTEUSE
The drums begin to roll!

A MAN
Citoyens, all!
We'll see best by the statue there!

ANOTHER [Pointing to **DE VARDES** and **THE MARQUISE**]
But these?—

THE FIRST
They're safe! Let them await our pleasure! Peste!
We waited once on theirs!

A THIRD
That's true!

[The **MOB** divides. **MEN** and **WOMEN** cluster about the base of the statue or upon the doorsteps of the surrounding houses. Enter **MEN** with banners.

THE MOB
Look! Look!
The painted banners! Vive la patrie!

SÉRAPHINE [To **THE MARQUISE**]
Hist!
Hist, madame! behind the pillar there!

[She points to the pillar of the church.

DE VARDES
Go!

[**THE MARQUISE** conceals herself behind the pillar.

[A crash of music.

[Enter **LALAIN** and **NANON**.

LALAIN
No blood to-day! I'd have clean sleep to-night,
Pure sleep and sweet, in which to dream of love!—
Hast seen her in her mantle blue?

NANON
Who stands
So steadfast there with a drawn sword?

LALAIN
Diable!

[He makes as if to cross to the church steps, where **DE VARDES**, sword in hand, stands with his back against a pillar. The **CROWD** comes between.

NANON
Patience, he'll not escape!

LALAIN [With affected indifference]
It is as well,—
To her he's but a ci-devant, and he,
O fool! shall see in her the Revolution!
Then, then, when she has passed, I'll deal with him!

[Singing within.

A VOICE
With sandals on her feet,
The Phrygian cap so red
Upon her sunny head,
She comes, she's coming sweet!
Reason, to whom we pay
All homage on this day!

THE CROWD
The singers! The actors!

[Enter **ACTORS** and **ACTRESSES** of the Theatre of Nantes, dressed as for the stage, and carrying garlands of paper flowers.

AN ACTOR
Way for Tartufe!
The Citizen Jourdain, Phèdre, Célimène,
Acaste, Armide, Aucassin, Nicolette!
Make way! Make way!

THE SINGER
Upon her lofty car
She sits in solemn state!
Of day the lovely mate,
Of night the shining star!
Reason, to whom we pay
All homage on this day!

THE CROWD
Brava! What now?

THE ACTOR
Voltaire, Rousseau, Franklin, Robespierre!

[Enter a band of **STUDENTS** drawing a garlanded float. Upon the float the busts of Voltaire, Rousseau, Franklin, and Robespierre.

THE CROWD
Vive Robespierre!

[The Marseillaise. Enter Republican **SOLDIERS**.

DE VARDES
Oh, for the red Hussars!

[Enter **FOUR MEN** wearing tricolour scarfs and plumes, huge cockades, pistols and sabres.

THE CROWD
The Commissioners!

DE VARDES
Hooded crows!

[There crosses the stage a float upon which is fixed a miniature guillotine.

THE CROWD
Ha! ha!
Vive la Guillotine!

A MAN
Vive les noyades!

DE VARDES
Cold
Are thy baths, O Apollo!

[Enter red-bonneted **MEN** and **WOMEN** dragging a tumbril in which are heaped spoils of the church,—broken images, crucifixes, candelabra, chalices, patens, etc.

THE CROWD
Ha—h—h!

DE VARDES
Jesu!

[He crosses himself.

[Music. The great tricolour flag of the Republic is borne across the stage.

THE CROWD
La patrie! Vive la patrie!

DE VARDES
France! France!

[Stately music. Enter young **MEN** in Greek dress, bearing a gilded framework upon which is fixed a tall flambeau, wreathed with flowers. They advance and place the structure before the church steps.

A PEASANT
Brave! But what is it?

ANOTHER
The torch of Reason!
The Goddess lights it,—then we worship her!

A THIRD
No, we worship Reason!

THE SECOND
'Tis the same thing!

[Enter young **GIRLS** clad in white, linked together with tricolour ribbons and carrying osier baskets from which they scatter flowers. They are followed by **CHILDREN** swinging censers, then by a shouting throng drawing a triumphal car upon which sits the Goddess of Reason. She is clothed in a white tunic and a blue mantle; upon her loosened hair is a wreath of oak leaves and she has in her hand a light spear.

THE CROWD
Reason! Reason!—Yvette! Yvette!

DE VARDES
Mon Dieu!

[The car stops.

[**YVETTE** rises.

THE CROWD
Vive la déesse! Vive Yvette!

[**LALAIN** comes forward.

Vive Lalain!

LALAIN
People of Nantes! Citoyens! Patriots!
Old things are past. To-day we welcome new.
Gone are the priests, gone is the crucifix;
Chalice and paten whelmed beneath the Loire!
Kings, princes, nobles, priests, all crumbled down!
Death on a pale horse hath ridden o'er them,
The ravens and the sea mews pick their bones.
Theirs are the yesterdays, the ci-devants!
The red to-day is ours, the purple morrow!—
Liberty, Equality, Fraternity!
We worship Thee, Triune and Indivisible!—
O Mother Nature, pure, beneficent,
Redeemed from darkness of the centuries,
Smile on thy children, come to worship thee!
And thou, supernal Reason, Crown of Man,
Eyes of the blind, divine, ascending flame,
Pearl without price, rose, light, music, warmth!—
O gushing spring where else were desert waste!
O flooding light, celestial melody!
O flower that blooms on either side the grave!
O steadfast star that burns the night away!
We worship thee!

[He takes the censer from a **BOY** and swings it to and fro before the standing goddess. Clouds of incense arise. The trumpets sound.

THE CROWD [With ecstasy]
We worship thee, Yvette!
Yvette! Yvette! Reason! Yvette Charruel!

YVETTE
O God! I knew not 'twas like this!

LALAIN
Reason, descend!
Illume thy torch, among us mortals dwell.
O sweetest Reason! ne'er regret the skies!
Descend—

[He gives his hand to **YVETTE**. She descends from the car.

A MAN
She is the fairest Reason!

ANOTHER
Now
She'll light the torch!

[A **BOY** brings her lighted touchwood.

[**LALAIN** fastens it to the point of her spear, and kneeling presents it to her. She advances to the church steps and raises the flaming lance in order to light the torch. She sees **DE VARDES**. The spear falls to the earth. The flame goes out.

YVETTE
O Our Lady!

THE CROWD
Light the torch! Light the torch!

LALAIN
What witchcraft's this?

YVETTE
None, none!—Oh, see the heavens open!

[Murmurs of the **CROWD**.

ANGÉLIQUE
Goddess!
Goddess!

CÉLISTE
She hears not!

THE CROWD
Light the torch!

LALAIN
I see
Hell gaping! What's that man to thee?
Death and damnation! Dost still gaze at him?
Then to the winds, Irresolution!

[He turns to the **CROWD**.

See,
Patriots, see! The light of Reason dies!
Out went the sacred flame beneath the eyes,
The basilisk eyes of an Aristocrat!

THE CROWD
Away with him to prison! Death! The Loire!
Death to the emigré!

[A rush toward the church steps. **DE VARDES** throws himself on guard. **YVETTE** comes between him and the **MOB**.

YVETTE
Back!

The Mob
Ah—h—h!

LALAIN
Art mad?
Stand from between the lion and his prey!

DE VARDES [To the **MOB**]
Men of Nantes! leave women to one side!
[To **YVETTE** with a gesture toward the car]
Goddess of Reason! Mount Olympus waits!
[To **LALAIN**]
At last, Rémond Lalain!

LALAIN
René de Vardes!

[A **MAN** strikes at **DE VARDES** with a long pike. His sword arm falls, and the sword rattles to the ground. A shout of triumph from the mob. **THE MARQUISE'S** cry from the pillar is not heard. The **MOB** moves forward.

YVETTE
Back, back, I say! You'll do no murder here!
What! One man against a score!—All Bretons!

THE MOB
Death to the emigré!

DE VARDES
Not emigré!
Good folk, I've been in prison in La Force.
Released, I journeyed home to Brittany!

A MAN
Thou'lt journey farther yet, Aristocrat!

ANGÉLIQUE
Thy boat shall travel down the Loire!

YVETTE
Shall it?
Shall it, indeed, thou gold-locked leprous woman!
Thy bark shall be sucked down by black Ahès!
I see three Vannetois!—big Rubik, Yann,
And Rivarol who won the singer's prize!
À moi, Vannetois!—Who is that standing there?
Huon! Rememberest thou the fields at dawn?
Rememberest thou the dim green hazel copse?
Rememberest thou one Pardon of Sainte Anne?

A PEASANT
Yvette!

YVETTE
The sun went down, the stars shone out;
We wandered round the wreckage of a ship;
Beneath a shell we found a golden coin.
Rememberest thou, Hervé the Cornouillaise?

A BRETON SAILOR
Yvette!

YVETTE
Baptiste! Michael! Monik! Ronan!
How loudly rang the bells of Quiberon!
To beat of drum we danced beside the sea!

YOUNG MEN
Ho, ho! That day!

YVETTE
Eh, who spoke to us there,
Of glory, of France, and of Liberty?
Citoyen Deputy Rémond Lalain!
Red wine he gave to you, to me a flower!
Mon Dieu! I was so proud—

LALAIN
Yvette!

YVETTE [To an **OLD WOMAN**]

Margot!
'Twas I who watched with thee one stormy night
When all thy seven sons were out at sea!

THE OLD WOMAN
Ay, ay, and they came safely home to me!

YVETTE [To a **CHILD**]
O little Jeanne, where is the doll I gave thee?

THE CHILD
Here!—'tis named 'Toinette!

A WOMAN [With the **CHILD**]
She has another
Named Yvette!

YVETTE [To a band of **YOUNG WOMEN**]
Fifine, Laure, and Veronique!
The moon shone bright, there was no wind at all,
Below the heights the violet shadows slept,
All sweetly smelled the gorse and white buckwheat,
And dewy was the grass beneath our feet,
And wet with dew the poppies in our hair!
There came a sound of singing from the sea,
Our hands we linked, we sped around Tantad,
Fair shone the moon—

A YOUNG GIRL
Oh, Eves of Saint John!

A BRETON
Lou! lou! An Tan! An Tan! An Tan!

SÉRAPHINE
Saint Ronan! Saint Primel!

THE CROWD
Yvette! Yvette!
Yvette Charruel!

YVETTE
O folk of Nantes!
There is a thing I want so badly, I!
Call it a fairing from the Fête of Reason,
And give the trifle to the poor Yvette,
The poor Yvette who's done her best to please you!
Oh, I've music made for you to dance by,

And for you held on high the great tricolour;
And in the night-time sung to you of dawn!
And for you, too, I've plucked the lilies up,
Fast locked a door and flung away the key,
And left the ravished garden evermore!—
A priest would say my soul I had imperilled.

THE CROWD
No, no! No priests! Reason! Reason! Yvette.

YVETTE
This mantle blue, these oak leaves in my hair,
These sandals and this spear, this tunic white,
The wreathèd car, the music and the song!
All, all a mockery, unless, unless—
There is a thing I want so badly, I!

A COMMISSIONER
It is thine!

THE CROWD
Thine! Thine! Yvette Charruel!

YVETTE
Ah, I would play the goddess, that I would!
I'd have my pardon like a Breton saint,
And what I bound, it should be bound indeed!
And what I loosed, it should be loosed indeed!

A COMMISSIONER
Fast bind or freely loose, thy surety, I!

ANOTHER
Command me, and the silver moon I'll bring thee!

YVETTE
With what a sudden glory shines the sun!
It gilds the streets, it gilds the running Loire!
And from them both the blood-stains fade away!
Ah, let us rest from death in Nantes to-day,
And think how falls the eve in Bethlehem!—
There is a little village that I know,
A hungry village by a hungry sea,
As worn and grey as any calvary!
The hungry shadows ate the sunshine up;
The children cried, the women wailed at morn;
The very Christ looked hungry on the Cross;
When lo! a miracle! for suddenly

The starving, haggard folk began to laugh,
The tender green put forth, the flowers bloomed,
Blue shone the sky, the lark sang overhead,
And mild the face of Christ and heavenly kind!
The little village had its fill of bread,
Yea, wine it drank, and cheerful breath it drew,
And, by the well, of this strange plenty talked,
Of tolls withdrawn, of perfect friendliness!

[She moves from before **DE VARDES**.

And then it blessed the man who gave it bread,
Who had a heart to feel with wretchedness,
And a strong arm to drive the hunger forth
As Arthur drove the giants from the land!
O men of Nantes! you'll keep your oath to me!
In Nantes to-day 'tis mine to loose or bind!—
I loose this man—

LALAIN
Out, witch!
[To **DE VARDES**]
Think not, think not,
René de Vardes, that she shall save thee thus!—
Mine, mine she is, she shall be, soul and all!

DE VARDES
Rémond Lalain—

LALAIN [To the **MOB**]
It is an emigré!
A traitor and a black Aristocrat,
The ci-devant De Vardes!

THE CROWD
De Vardes! De Vardes!

YVETTE
Rémond Lalain, stand from my path, I say!
[To the **CROWD**]
Not emigré, but prisoner in La Force!
Not traitor! That's a wretch who doth betray!
Aristocrat?—Who chooseth his birth star?
Crieth at Life's gate, "Of such an house I'm heir!"
But in we drift from the great sea without;
A current takes us—"Of my house are ye!"
So you, so I, so this citoyen here,
Rémond Lalain, who is Lalain by chance,

And might have been Capet or Mirabeau!
And so this other, standing gravely there
Alone, a man alone upon a rock,
And the tide mounts!—The current swept him there!
Another drift, and he had been Lalain,
Orator and idol of the Jacobins!—
Names! They are the mist through which the man
Is scarce discerned, the sea-drift hides the pearl.
Ghosts of the past the present spurns! Dead leaves!
Masks for the pauper and the prince! Mere names!
I would not have them rule my spirit thus!—
Aristocrat! I know not, but I know
The man's been known to lift a peasant's load
And gather seaweed with a fisher's child!

A BRETON SOLDIER
'Tis true! And in my boat he's been with me,
When Ahès and the storm made black the sea!

A PEASANT
He walked beside me in the field and told
Name of the silver star above the fold!

A SOLDIER
I was a red Hussar! He fought like Mars.
Eh, my Colonel—

A WOMAN
We know, we Morbec folk!
Vive Baron René!

SÉRAPHINE
Eh, eh, monseigneur!

YVETTE
Nantes! Nantes! you'll keep the oath you've made to me!
My fairing I shall have this holiday,
And what I bind it shall be bound indeed,
And what I loose is loosed to me for aye!
I ask one gift—I shall not ask again!
This is my hour, no other hour I want.
I ask one life—is't mine, is't mine, Citoyens?

THE CROWD
Yes, yes! 'Tis thine!

A COMMISSIONER
Thine, Goddess!

[To **DE VARDES**]
Citoyen, thou art free!

LALAIN
Diable!

YVETTE
I'm faint.—

SÉRAPHINE
Saint Iguinou! What of the pillar there?

A COMMISSIONER
Make way for the Citoyen Vardes!

THE CROWD
Make way!

SÉRAPHINE
Eh, eh, monseigneur; thou hadst best begone!

DE VARDES [to **THE COMMISSIONER**]
Citoyen, thanks! but here I'll watch awhile
These pleasing rites, this worship new of Reason!

THE COMMISSIONER
'Twill do thee good, Aristocrat!

DE VARDES
No doubt,
Citoyen!

LALAIN
Oh, depth of hell!

NANON
Oh, patience!

LALAIN
Why takes he not his liberty? He stays!
To feast his eyes upon her face he stays!
Diable! He speaks to her—

NANON
Patience! Patience!—
What flutters there behind the pillar?

LALAIN

Where?

[She points. They move together to the base of the statue.

DE VARDES [To **YVETTE**]
I owe my life to thee, thou hapless child!
Ah, couldst thou make this throng depart the place!

YVETTE
Monseigneur—

THE CROWD
Goddess of Reason! light the torch!

YVETTE
I'm faint!—The houses all are dancing there!—
Give me drink!

A MAN
Here's wine!

[He pours wine into a great gold cup.

YVETTE
'Tis in a chalice!

THE CROWD
Drink!

[**YVETTE** drinks.

YVETTE
Nom de Dieu! 'Tis right good wine, indeed!—
Not now I'll light the torch—'Tis out for good!
And while we linger here the sunlight goes!
Let's to the quai, let's to the quai and dance—
And dance the Carmagnole!

THE CROWD
The Carmagnole!

[**MEN** and **WOMEN** take hands and begin to dance.

YVETTE
Away! Down the long street, and to the quai!
Take hands! Away! Dansons la Carmagnole!

[She snatches from a **BOY** a tambourine and strikes it.

Vive le son, vive le son,
Vive le son du canon!

[**THE CROWD** disperses. **DE VARDES** remains standing before the pillar behind which crouches **THE MARQUISE. SÉRAPHINE** watches from the church steps;

[**LALAIN** and **NANON** from the base of the Statue of Liberty.

Monseigneur!

DE VARDES
Ay.

YVETTE
Now, now while the lark sings,
And while the fairy wood is green, begone!
Oh, 'tis not safe in Nantes! They gave thy life,
But oh, they're fierce and fickle! Back they'll come!
I've enemies in Nantes, and there's Lalain,
Rémond Lalain who'll work me woe at last!
Thou must begone, but list, ah, list to me!
I know a secret place where thou mayst bide,
So safe! so safe! and I will bring thee food,
White bread and wine, and find for thee a way
Forth from the town—

DE VARDES
Ah, I may trust thee, sure!

YVETTE
I never knew thou wast in prison there!
So sad, so dark the prison life, they say!
My cagèd bird I freed the other day.
There are so many prisoners in Nantes,
I would not have it one!—

DE VARDES
My life I owe—

YVETTE
The spring draws on; 'twill soon be June again!

DE VARDES
Now for another life I make my suit—

YVETTE
In Paimpont Wood the trees are greening now,

In sun and shade the purple violets blow!

DE VARDES
In those old convent days, ah, ages gone!
Beneath the fruit trees, by the fountain there,
I've seen thee nurse a little fluttering bird,
Wounded and frightened, fallen from the blue,
But yet God's bird, and with a life to save!
And thou didst stroke its plumage tenderly,
And gently fostered it between thy hands
Awhile, and up it soared into the blue;
A moment since and thou didst save my life.
Lo now, there is another thing to do!
Before my own life, I've a life in charge,
And to thee now I turn, and plead for help.
In this wild town thou rulest o'er the hour;
Be now the goddess and the woman too,
Pitiful, tender, generous, and true!—
Lo! here a wounded bird—

[He moves aside. **THE MARQUISE** leaves the shadow of the pillar.

YVETTE
Death of my life!

THE MARQUISE
Oh, guard me, all ye saints!

DE VARDES
Yvette! Yvette!

[**LALAIN** comes forward from the statue.

LALAIN [To **YVETTE**]
Right of the Seigneur!

YVETTE
So! Thou hast returned,
Beneath the trees, along the moonlit road!
And in thine arms the rose and eglantine,
And on thy lips the song of all the birds!
Back! There is a furze field bars thy way!

THE MARQUISE
Mon Dieu!

YVETTE
Hast thou another fan to break?

Ha! shrinkest thou?

THE MARQUISE
Sainte Geneviève!

YVETTE [Raising her voice]
Nantes! Nantes!

DE VARDES
By all the gods!—

YVETTE
À moi! À moi! Nantes!

[An answering cry from within.

DE VARDES
Herd girl of Morbec—

LALAIN
Right of the Seigneur!

YVETTE
À moi! Citoyens! Patriots!

[Re-enter **MOB**.

DE VARDES
Courage,
Clarice!

THE MARQUISE
O all ye saints!

YVETTE
Citoyens!
This ci-devant, this black Aristocrat!
Oh! all this while she was in hiding here!
Beside the pillar there she kneeled and laughed.
Do I not know her laughter, rippling sweet
Or o'er a broken fan or broken heart,
Or in green Morbec and a garden fair,
Or on the moonlit road to ancient Vannes?—
She, she the ci-devant, the emigrée!
Who to false England with her jewels fled,—
Rubies, emeralds, and long strings of pearls!
The while in barren fields her peasants starved!—
I denounce the Citoyenne Blanchefôret!

THE CROWD
Ah—h—h!

THE MARQUISE
O terror!

DE VARDES
Thy hand in mine, Clarice!

YVETTE
What of, what of the dark line of De Vardes?
What tales are told of Morbec's black château?
More wicked and more lost than sunken Ys!
Wolves were they all, the seigneurs of Morbec!
Henri, Philippe, Gil, René, Amaury—
All, all were wolves who lurked, who sprang, who tore,
No heart of lamb, but just the heart of man!
Heart of a man, heart of a woman too!
Morbec! De Vardes! No direr names in France!
Right hands of kings, priests, soldiers, cardinals,
Courtiers and lovers of the fleur-de-lis!
Passionate, proud, a whirlwind and a flame!
Morbec! De Vardes! 'Ware all who came between
The whirlwind and its goal, the stubble and the flame!

DE VARDES
Thou lost soul!

LALAIN
Thou lovely fiend!

YVETTE
De Vardes! De Vardes! The name comes on the blast
Up from the gulf where lie the thrones of kings.
Battle, oppression, tyranny and wrong—
Miramand, Blanchefôret! on sea winds in they float
From that dim palace where that lost Ahès
Down to her emerald windows beckons man
And spreads the bridal bed in sunken Ys!

NANON
Mon Dieu! The bridal bed!

YVETTE
By all the wrongs
That both their houses through the ages long
Have wrought us! By the blood that they have shed,

The tears, the groans, the sweat, the servile knees,
The bitter bread they gave us, and the cry
From lonely graves of anguish and of wrath!
By all the hunger and the freezing cold!
By all the toil and all the hopelessness,
The smitten cheek, the taunt, the burning heart!
By all the Rights of all the Lords of Wrong!
By Corvée and Gabelle and Gibier,
Quintaines, Milods, Ban d'Août and Bordelage,
Fouage, Leide, Corvée à miséricorde,
Banvin, Chansons, Baiser des Mariées!
I do denounce these two Aristocrats:
La Force's prisoner, and the emigrée,
La belle Marquise, the Hussar of the King,
Citoyen Vardes, Citoyenne Blanchefôret!

LALAIN
So!

THE MOB
Away! Away! Prison! Death! The Loire!
Down, down, Aristocrats.

[They close around **DE VARDES** and **THE MARQUISE**.

SÉRAPHINE
Saint Maturin!
Saint Corentin! Saint Jean!

THE MARQUISE
O bitter death!

DE VARDES
I am thy death, who thought to save thee so!

[The **SOLDIERS** lay hands upon **DE VARDES** and **THE MARQUISE** and force them from the church steps and across the square.

THE MOB
Away!

A COMMISSIONER
The nearest prison!

A MAN
That's the Church
Of Saint Eustache!

A COMMISSIONER
Away! They shall be judged
By Carrier!

THE MOB
Carrier!—The Loire!

YVETTE
Ah!

ANGÉLIQUE
Ha, ha! Le Mariage Républicain!

YVETTE
Quoi!

ANGÉLIQUE
Eh, they're lovers, are they not?

CÉLISTE
The Loire shall marry them, the ci-devants!

ANGÉLIQUE
Yvette has made the wedding, eh, Yvette?

THE MOB
Ha, ha! Le Mariage Républicain!

[Exeunt the **MOB**, **SOLDIERS**, **DE VARDES**, and **THE MARQUISE**, guarded, etc.

VOICES [Within]
Le Mariage Républicain! Ha, ha!

YVETTE
What have I done?—

VOICES [Dying away]
Ha, ha! ha, ha! The Loire!

YVETTE
The Loire!—O God!

CURTAIN

The interior of a church in Nantes used as a prison. Great broken windows of stained glass, purple and crimson, through which streams the sunlight. Prisoners of both sexes and all ages and conditions of life move to and fro, or lean against the pillars which support the vaulted roof. Some rest or kneel upon the steps before the altar rail. Three children play beside a broken font. Against a door at the left of the great altar lounge several turnkeys dressed in blue woollen with red liberty caps.

THE MARQUISE sits beside a pillar. She talks with **DE BUC** and **ENGUERRAND LA FÔRET**. Near her are **COUNT LOUIS** and **MLLE. DE CHÂTEAU-GUI**. **DE L'ORIENT** stands upon a bench beneath a shattered window. **DE VARDES** sits at a rude table writing.

A butterfly enters at the broken window and flutters through the church.

A CHILD
The butterfly! The butterfly!

MLLE. DE CHÂTEAU-GUI
Oh, see
Its painted wings!

A CHILD
There! There!

MLLE. DE CHÂTEAU-GUI
It comes my way!—I've caught it!—No!

AN ACTRESS [Dressed as a shepherdess]
I!
I have it fast, the pretty prisoner!

DE L'ORIENT
It will not stay—

COUNT LOUIS
It soars into the roof!
No! down again on yon long ray of light!—
Give chase!

DE L'ORIENT
Here!

MLLE. DE CHÂTEAU-GUI
There!

THE ACTRESS
Oh, oh! It sails this way,
The fairy boat—

DE L'ORIENT

With freight of heart's desire!

THE ACTRESS
I have it!

COUNT LOUIS
No, I!

[The butterfly lights upon his hand.

'Tis youth!

DE L'ORIENT
'Tis gone!—

[The butterfly brushes his shoulder.

'Tis joy!

THE ACTRESS
Fled!—Ah, ah!—'Tis hope!

[The butterfly touches her outstretched arm, then rises again.

No longer!

[The butterfly rests upon the fair hair of **THE MARQUISE**.

THE MARQUISE
As I was saying, then I felt despair—

[The butterfly rises, flutters in a shaft of sunshine, then passes out of the window. The **PRISONERS** watch its flight.

A CHILD
The butterfly has gone!

MLLE. DE CHÂTEAU-GUI
Whither!

DE L'ORIENT
'Tis for
The blue skies and the sunny fields!

THE ACTRESS
The flowers
We shall not gather any more!

DE L'ORIENT
High hills,
The water running in the sun and shade!

MME. DE MALESTROIT
A garden old beside a winding stream—
Oh, death in life!

A NUN
It was a soul set free.
By now a thousand shining leagues it's mounted!

[The door at the left of the altar opens.

[Enter **GRÉGOIRE**.

MLLE. DE CHÂTEAU-GUI
Here is Grégoire!

GRÉGOIRE
Good-morrow, Citoyens!

COUNT LOUIS
Good-morrow, Gaoler.

MLLE. DE CHÂTEAU-GUI
Ah, this place, Grégoire!
It is so triste! Shall we forever stay
Imprisoned in a church?

LA FÔRET
Oh, gayer far
The Bastille or Vincennes!

THE ACTRESS
These frowning saints!
The wind that whistles in!

MME. DE MALESTROIT
The stones so cold!

COUNT LOUIS
The Church will make us martyrs ere our time!

MLLE. DE CHÂTEAU-GUI
And did you buy, Grégoire, the cards for ombre?

THE ACTRESS

Masks for our play?

DE L'ORIENT
A violin?

THE ACTRESS
Wax-lights?

DE BUC
The foils?

A CHILD
My ball, Grégoire?

GRÉGOIRE
I've nothing bought—
The judges sit to-day. Complain to them.
The church is cold! 'Tis not so cold as Loire!
The prisons are too crowded! Well, to-day
We'll weed them out!

DE BUC
So!

GRÉGOIRE
You are warned! Prepare!
Make your farewells—the time is very short!

[Exit **GRÉGOIRE**.

DE BUC
Strike camp!

DE L'ORIENT
The open road!

COUNT LOUIS
Who goes?

LA FÔRET
Who stays?

MLLE. DE CHÂTEAU-GUI
Our comedy!—we cannot have it now!

THE ACTRESS
Oh, we will rearrange the parts!

[**DE VARDES** folds his letter and rises from the table.

DE VARDES
We'll play,
Though all the world is sliding 'neath our feet!

DE BUC
The world's a stage—

THE NUN
De profundis clamavi
Ad te Domine!

[Enter **THE ABBÉ** Jean de Barbasan, pale, wounded, and with disordered dress.

MLLE. DE CHÂTEAU-GUI
Monsieur l'Abbé!

DE VARDES
Ah!
De Barbasan, we feared for you!

THE ABBÉ
Morbleu!
I am reprieved! Lambertye proved my friend!
It seems that once I saved the villain's life!—
Pure accident!—stumbled on him in a ditch,
Played the Samaritan!—so now I'm spared,
Come forth like Daniel from the lions' den,
That Judgment Hall of theirs across the way!
Lions! They are not lions, they are wolves,
Hyenas, tigers, and baboons. Faugh!

DE BUC
So!
They are hungry yet?

THE ABBÉ
Oh, they are portents!
And portents are the folk that fill that hall!
Not women they who sit aloft and knit;
Not men, those scarecrow visages below;
For robed judges, wolves at Lammas tide,
And Nantes the winter forest for the pack!—
But ah, the deer at bay, the little lambs!—
The earth gives 'neath their feet, they face the Loire!

[A confused sound from the square without the window; **VOICES**, menacing and execrating, a cry, then silence.

DE VARDES
One has not gained the Loire!

THE ABBÉ
Ah, oftentimes,
They fall before they reach the Judgment Hall!
There in the street, before that fatal door—
Both youth and age, fair women and brave men.
Their blood cries to another judgment seat!
From yonder window you may see it all!

THE MARQUISE
We will not look!

COUNT LOUIS
Fie, fie, De Barbasan!
There is a time for everything! Not now,
Nor in this place is't meet or debonair
To speak of ravening wolves or stricken deer!
To work, my friend! You find us much concerned
About this play of Molière's! We give
Le Bourgeois Gentilhomme.

THE MARQUISE
You'll play Jourdain?
Béjart had promised us, but then he went.
He's not returned.

THE ABBÉ
Nor will, I think. But, yes,
I'll take the part; I'll speak in prose to you
To whom I else would speak in poetry!

THE MARQUISE [With a curtesy]
Monsieur Jourdain, your prose is ravishing!—
I'm Dorimène.

DE BUC
And I Dorante!

MLLE. DE CHÂTEAU-GUI
Lucille.

MME. DE MALESTROIT
Nicole!

THE ACTRESS
I am, Monsieur Jourdain, your wife!

LA FÔRET
Your son-in-law the Turk!

DE VARDES
Behold, monsieur,
Your fencing master!

DE L'ORIENT
Your maître de danse.
Imagine, pray, you hear my violin:
La, la—The minuet!—La, la, la!

[He plays an imaginary violin. The **PRISONERS** hesitate, laugh, then begin to step a minuet. The **CHILDREN** and the **GAOLERS** watch them. **DE VARDES** does not dance. He leans against a pillar to the left. Enter a **TURNKEY**, **CÉLISTE**, **ANGÉLIQUE**, **NANON**, and **SÉRAPHINE**.

SÉRAPHINE [Crossing herself]
Eh! Eh! They dance!—Well, what a thing it is
To be a noble born!

CÉLISTE [Jealously]
We dance as well!

SÉRAPHINE
Ay, the Carmagnole!

ANGÉLIQUE
'Tis a swifter dance!
Why came we here? I never liked this church,
They are too gay of heart, these ci-devants!
Let's to the Judgment Hall, or to the Loire.

CÉLISTE
Séraphine would come—

SÉRAPHINE
Patience, Citoyennes,
No haste! I've just a little word to speak
Unto monseigneur there.

CÉLISTE
Monseigneur!

SÉRAPHINE

Oh,
The Citoyen Vardes! You know my tripping tongue.

NANON [To **THE TURNKEY**]
Where is that ci-devant men once did call
La belle Marquise?

THE TURNKEY
'Tis she who dances there,
Fair-haired and dressed in violet.

NANON
Awhile
I'll watch her dance.

CÉLISTE
Their cheeks are pale.

ANGÉLIQUE
They smile.
I would not smile if I were they.

[**NANON**, **CÉLISTE**, and **ANGÉLIQUE** watch the **DANCERS**. **SÉRAPHINE** approaches **DE VARDES**.

SÉRAPHINE [In a low voice]
Monseigneur!

DE VARDES
Séraphine Robin, I believe?

SÉRAPHINE
Saint Yves!
Now just to think! Monseigneur knows my name!—
Eh! Morbec was my home for many a year.
When all is said and done, Home is just Home,
Hut or château—and always the De Vardes
Were lords of Morbec did they good or ill!
Most like 'twas ill—but they were proper men!
And when they smiled we always said 'twas day;
And old men say—but it was long ago—
A baron lived was named René the Good!
Saint Gil! Monseigneur gave us back Lisette.
Saint Maudez! 'Tis a dangerous thing, but see!

[She takes from her bosom a silken purse.

Eh, monseigneur, 'tis yours! Take it! Quick, quick,
Before Céleste—the baggage!—turns her head!

[She thrusts the purse into his hand.

DE VARDES
From whom?

SÉRAPHINE
Look in it! You will see. 'Tis gold.

DE VARDES
Gold!

SÉRAPHINE
And something more.—Here is Angélique!

ANGÉLIQUE
Aristocrat—That ring upon thy finger—

SÉRAPHINE
Out!

DE VARDES
Not yet, Citoyenne!

ANGÉLIQUE
Then afterwards!
I'll have it at the trenches or the Loire!

[She rejoins **CÉLISTE** and **NANON**. They watch the **DANCERS**.

DE L'ORIENT
Nicole—Lucille—Cléonte—

SÉRAPHINE
My errand's done—
Look in the purse, monseigneur, look at once!

DE L'ORIENT
La, la, la, la!

DE VARDES
I have no need of gold.

SÉRAPHINE
Look, monseigneur!

DE VARDES
Again, from whom?

SÉRAPHINE
A friend.

DE VARDES
I have no friend in Nantes. Take back thy purse!

SÉRAPHINE
It is not mine, the pretty, silken thing!
I swore that I would leave it, so I will!
And I was told to tell you, "Look within."

[**NANON** approaches.

NANON
In Nantes one is Suspect when one is seen
Whispering in shadows with Aristocrats!

SÉRAPHINE
Nothing I said you might not hear, Nanon!
Come, come away!
[To **DE VARDES** as she turns from him]
Monseigneur, have a care!

[**SÉRAPHINE**, **NANON**, **CÉLISTE**, and **ANGÉLIQUE** watch the **DANCERS**. A grating sound is heard without the door to the left of the altar. The turnkeys move aside, the door opens and discloses a passage lined with **GAOLERS** and **SOLDIERS**.

[Enter **GRÉGOIRE** with three or four Patriots. They wear great boots, plumed hats, sashes of tricolour, sabres and pistols.

DE L'ORIENT
La, la, la, la, la!

GRÉGOIRE
The list for the day.

[The dance ceases.

CÉLISTE
Now, now we'll see the birds drop one by one!

ANGÉLIQUE
It is what I love!

GRÉGOIRE [He descends the step from the choir]
The list, Citoyens!
You whom I name pass out at yonder door.

Across the square the judges sit—

DE BUC
Just so!
Who leads?

GRÉGOIRE
Citoyen, you!

DE BUC
Promotion, by God!—
Messieurs, mesdames, I have marching orders!
[To **THE ACTRESS** and **MLLE. DE CHÂTEAU-GUI**]
I cannot play Dorante! Is't not a shame?
De L'Orient there must take my part—Adieu!
[To **THE MARQUISE**]
Ah, Dorimène, you'll let me kiss your hand?

THE MARQUISE
Monsieur, monsieur—

DE BUC [To **DE VARDES**]
I'm breaking camp.

DE VARDES
Ma foi!
We'll meet at the end of the march, my friend!
Meantime I'll tell thee that Bouillé once said,
"Brave as a Gascon, or Fauquemont de Buc!"

DE BUC
Did he so? Old Bouillé!

[He salutes.

My Colonel!

DE VARDES
Captain de Buc!

[**DE BUC** mounts the step into the choir and passes out of the door, between the lines of **SOLDIERS**. There is heard the voice of the **MOB** in the square without.

DE L'ORIENT
Away with Melancholy!
The curtain's up, the play begins! Grégoire,
My name is Thalia! Is't on thy list?

GRÉGOIRE [His eyes upon the paper in his hand]
No, Citoyen.

DE L'ORIENT
Another lifetime here!

COUNT LOUIS
A golden louis to a paper franc,
The next is Château-Gui!—

GRÉGOIRE
No, Château-Gui,
You are reserved.

COUNT LOUIS [Taking snuff]
Why, that is welcome news!
Eh, my daughter, we will not miss the play!

GRÉGOIRE
The Citoyen Charles Le Blanc.

LE BLANC
What damned star
Flared and went out the night that I was born?

[Exit **LE BLANC**.

GRÉGOIRE
Hervé Rauderendec, called the Breton!

THE BRETON
Good people all, it has been pleasant here,
But now the tide draws to the full—Adieu!
I must make sail!

[Exit **THE BRETON**.

GRÉGOIRE
The Citoyenne Gérard.

THE ACTRESS
I?

GRÉGOIRE
Delphine Gérard.

THE ACTRESS
Oh, I knew, I knew

The butterfly that touched me was ill luck!
I named it Hope,—it fled, it fled away!

THE ABBÉ
We're loth to let you go, Delphine Gérard.

THE ACTRESS
There is no choice—I have my cue, you see!—
And after all the play's a tragedy.

[Exit **THE ACTRESS**.

CÉLISTE
'Tis better worth our while across the square!

ANGÉLIQUE
'Tis so! Let's to the Judgment Hall.

NANON
Agreed.
Come, Séraphine!

SÉRAPHINE
I'll follow presently.

ANGÉLIQUE
Do not delay. We'll keep a place for you!

[Exeunt **NANON**, **CÉLISTE**, and **ANGÉLIQUE**.

GRÉGOIRE
The Citoyenne Vaucourt.

MME. DE VAUCOURT
Children, children!
Your father's calling me from Paradise!—
Thérèse, Philippe, farewell, farewell, farewell!
Oh, clasp me close and kiss!—Forget me not!—
Yes, yes, I'll buy the bonbons and the doll!
I'll not forget—

GRÉGOIRE
The boy goes with you.

MME. DE VAUCOURT [Wildly]
With me! He's but a babe! Not eight till June!

THE BOY [Clinging to her]

To the toy-shop, mother!

MME. DE VAUCOURT
Oh, yes, child, yes!
To the toy-shop!

[They go out together.

GRÉGOIRE
Maria Innocenta Sombreuil!

[A young **GIRL** in the habit of a Carmelite novice leaves the shadow of a pillar, with raised face and hands crossed upon her breast mounts the step and passes out between the **SOLDIERS**.

Gaspard Le Borgne!

LE BORGNE
An angel leads me on.

[He follows the novice.

GRÉGOIRE
Enguerrand La Fôret!

LA FÔRET
Ha, ha!—ha, ha!
Ha, ha!—

[Hysterical and continued laughter. **GRÉGOIRE** and the **TURNKEYS** look stolidly on, but the **PRISONERS** are disturbed.

COUNT LOUIS
For shame, Enguerrand La Fôret!
Before women!—Die like a gentleman!

LA FÔRET [He leans against the balustrade of the choir]
Ha, ha!

COUNT LOUIS
Fie, fie! You shame us all!

LA FÔRET
Ha, ha!
I laugh because—ha, ha!—'tis such a joke!

[He mounts the step still laughing, then suddenly recovers himself and turns with fury.

Who calls me coward? I laughed because I laughed!

[He wrests a musket from the nearest **SOLDIER** and stabs him with the bayonet.

Take that!—There's one at least will laugh no more!

[Oaths and confusion among the gaolers and soldiers. A sigh of satisfaction from the prisoners. **LA FÔRET** is dragged out. **GRÉGOIRE** looks at his list, then at **DE VARDES**. The latter advances.

GRÉGOIRE [Hurriedly to himself]
To-morrow—not to-day! I'll risk that much,—
Just for the way he fought that Morbec night!
[Aloud]
Stand back, Citoyen Vardes! Your time's not yet.

[A murmur of pleasure and congratulation from the **PRISONERS**.

MLLE. DE CHÂTEAU-GUI
We are so pleased, Monsieur le Baron!

GRÉGOIRE
Citoyens Rochedagon and Pincornet!

[The **MEN** named go out. There is heard from the square without and from the passage a sound of acclamation. The door is flung open and **THE ACTRESS** enters.

THE ACTRESS
They harmed me not! "No, no!" they said. "No, no!
Delphine Gérard must play for us in Nantes."
Oh, the people! Oh, the dear good people!
Oh, blessed fortune!

DE VARDES
We are most happy!

THE ABBÉ
Delphine Gérard!

COUNT LOUIS
Welcome, mademoiselle!
You see the play is still a comedy!

GRÉGOIRE
Marneil, Delille!

[Exeunt the **MEN** named.

DE L'ORIENT
The leaves fall fast,

The tree will soon be bare!

GRÉGOIRE
The Citoyenne
Clarice-Marie Miramand Blanchefôret.

DE VARDES
Oh, wretch!

THE PRISONERS
La belle Marquise!

THE MARQUISE
It is my name!—
I had no thought I would be called to-day!—
Unwarned! That's horrible! Ah, good Grégoire!
A little while—

GRÉGOIRE [Stolidly]
Citoyenne Blanchefôret.

THE MARQUISE
Ah, villain!

DE VARDES [To **GRÉGOIRE**]
Five minutes!

[He slips into **GRÉGOIRE**'s hand the purse of gold. **GRÉGOIRE** hesitates a moment, then his hand closes upon the purse. He thrusts it into his bosom.

SÉRAPHINE
Saint Michel!

[**DE VARDES** comes to **THE MARQUISE** and they speak together. **GRÉGOIRE** turns to another group of **PRISONERS**.

GRÉGOIRE
Montfauçon and Guistelles.

SÉRAPHINE
Saint Guenolé!
He hath the purse! The paper in it too!
He's rock; he, black Grégoire! Alack the day!
Saint Huon! What's to do?—

GRÉGOIRE
Sorel and Mornay!

SÉRAPHINE
Saint Yves le Véridique! I will away!

[Exit **SÉRAPHINE**.

DE VARDES [To **THE MARQUISE**]
Would I might die for thee!

THE MARQUISE
'Tis but a dream!

DE VARDES
Clarice! Clarice!

THE MARQUISE
A vision of the night!

DE VARDES
Clarice-Marie!

THE MARQUISE
I will awake!

DE VARDES
My friend!

THE MARQUISE
Ah, only that!

DE VARDES
La belle Marquise!

THE MARQUISE
No more!

DE VARDES
How long have we been friends! And now—

THE MARQUISE
And now!—

DE VARDES
My friend, my friend!

THE MARQUISE
Alas! Alas, 'tis true
We are good friends—in life and death good friends!
'Tis much—though there are lovers too in Nantes,

And when one loves 'tis not so hard to die!
Or so I've heard, monsieur.

DE VARDES
O destiny!

THE MARQUISE
The jasmine is my flower—a luckless bloom!
Wear not the too-sweet jasmine flower,
For then one loves, but is not loved again!

DE VARDES
No, no! the rose—

THE MARQUISE
The rose unloved! Ay, ay!
Last night I dreamed of roses and of lights,
Beside a water still they burned and bloomed—
Lit candles and pale roses with gold hearts,
Like those that bloomed within my garden once,
When you rode by, when you rode by, my friend!

DE VARDES
Alas!

THE MARQUISE
They're dead, my garden roses, dead!
They'll bloom no more, nor wilt thou ride that way;
Nor, Sieur de Morbec, dost thou love the rose.
For once thou said'st to me upon a day
When I did find the Morbec roses fair,
"I better love the heartsease at thy feet."
The peasant flower! Rememb'rest thou that day?
'Twas Saint John's Eve—

DE VARDES
Would I remembered not!

THE MARQUISE
The heartsease—

DE VARDES
The heartsease withered.

[A roar from the square. **DE L'ORIENT** turns from the window.

DE L'ORIENT
Ah!

COUNT LOUIS
What do you see?

DE L'ORIENT
Too much!

[A **TURNKEY** laughs.

THE TURNKEY
Carrier! Lalain!
Oh, they judge quickly! Vive la République!

THE MARQUISE
It was a summer day when first we met,
And now we part within a prison here,
And never shall we see each other more!

DE VARDES
Oh, briefer than the fairest summer day
The little hour before we meet again!
Soon, soon I'll follow thee, and all of these!
The reaper hath his sickle in the corn.
He is a madman, but the field is God's,
And God will garner up the fallen ears,
And in another life we two shall meet!

THE MARQUISE
And wilt thou love me then? Ah, no! Ah, no!

DE VARDES
Thou art a lady brave and fair—

THE MARQUISE
Alas!

GRÉGOIRE
The Nun Benôite, an Ursuline!

[A **NUN** rises from her knees, makes the sign of the cross, and passes out between the **SOLDIERS**.

THE MARQUISE
Ah me!
The unknown land, just guessed at and no more,
To which this loud wind sends my cockle boat!—
Where are my beads? Lost, lost with all things else!
Jewels and gold and friends and lovers too!—
Ah, short my shrift with Grégoire glowering there.

My hatred of Madame la Maréchale,
I'm sorry for't. The Captal de Montgis
Once did me wrong. Well, well, I can forgive!—
Sieur de Morbec, where's she that flung us down,
Lifted her finger and behold us here!
Her face is fair—ah, very fair her face.
She was your mistress, yes?

DE VARDES
No!

THE MARQUISE
What then?

DE VARDES
Cold that I warmed, and hunger that I fed.

THE MARQUISE
O strike her, Frost! O Hunger, with her wed!

DE VARDES
Ah, curse her not! She knew not what she did!

THE MARQUISE
Alas! Alas!

GRÉGOIRE
The Citoyenne L'Esparre!

THE MARQUISE
The women go—He'll call my name! Ah, look!
The purple saints within the windows there,
See how they wave their palms and smile at me!
They wave their palms, they strike their golden harps,
Their aureoles are brighter than the sun!

GRÉGOIRE
The Citoyenne Blanchefôret!

THE MARQUISE
The clock has struck!

DE VARDES
All angels guard thee!

THE MARQUISE
Fatal is my name
And hated through long years in Brittany.

Perhaps I shall not live to cross the square!

[The noise of the **MOB** without.

Oh, hear!

DE VARDES
Take courage!

THE MARQUISE
From the window there,
Wilt watch me on my way?

DE VARDES
Ay!

GRÉGOIRE
Citoyenne!

THE MARQUISE
Farewell! Ah, not my hand, my friend!

DE VARDES [He kisses her upon the brow]
Farewell!
Farewell—

[**THE MARQUISE** turns to the remaining prisoners.

THE MARQUISE
Messieurs, mesdames, 'tis with regret
I take my leave of this fair company!
My part of Dorimène—it must be played
By some more able, not more willing, one;
For me—I'm bidden to a wider stage.
Adieu! Adieu! Adieu!

THE PRISONERS
La belle Marquise!

[Exit **THE MARQUISE**. **DE VARDES** crosses to the window. **DE L'ORIENT** gives him place, and he stands upon the bench and watches the square without.

COUNT LOUIS
There are three names that most of all they hate:
De Vardes and Château-Gui and Blanchefôret!

GRÉGOIRE
Pasquier, Harlebeque, and Damazan.

[There is heard from the street without a confused sound of execration and triumph. The now small company of **PRISONERS** exchange glances.

DE VARDES [At the window]
Grand Dieu!

DE L'ORIENT [Beside him]
They dare not!—Ah!

[The sound without grows to a roar.

COUNT LOUIS
What seest thou?

DE L'ORIENT
Malediction!

[A cry without. **DE VARDES**, at the window, raises his voice.

DE VARDES
Clarice! Clarice!

[There is a faint answering cry, followed by a roar from the **MOB**, then silence.

MLLE. DE CHÂTEAU-GUI
O Ciel!

THE ACTRESS
Miséricorde!

DE VARDES
'Tis done—'tis past—she's dead.
O God who makest man, forbear, forbear!

[He covers his face with his hands. There is a silence. **GRÉGOIRE** folds his papers.

COUNT LOUIS [With a shaking voice]
'Tis well with her at last; we need not weep.
We all must die, for so the play goes on!
Her father was a lord of Gascony;
A golden spur he wore, and loved the chase!
Her mother was more fair than Montespan.
A thousand times we've hunted with the King,
De Miramand and I; a thousand times
We've watched the moon, that first Clarice and I!

GRÉGOIRE

To-morrow, at this hour, another list!
Meantime, Citoyens, you and you and you,
And you, Citoyennes, who petitioned so,
Your prayer is heard. Lalain is merciful!
You shall not sleep on these cold stones to-night,
Another gaol's provided. Follow me!

MLLE. DE CHÂTEAU-GUI
O welcome change!

COUNT LOUIS
The stones were very cold!

THE ACTRESS
And can we have our play there just the same?

GRÉGOIRE
Just the same.

[The **PRISONERS** move toward the door. **DE VARDES** touches **GRÉGOIRE** on the arm.

DE VARDES
I find the stones no colder than their wont,
Time moves no heavier here than everywhere,
And here, Grégoire, I will remain. The Church
Will give me up when Carrier calls my name!

DE L'ORIENT
I will keep you company—

GRÉGOIRE
As you will—
To-morrow you'll be called—you have one night.
[To the other **PRISONERS**]
Follow me.

[Exeunt all but **DE VARDES** and **DE L'ORIENT**. The latter flings himself upon the bench beneath the window; **DE VARDES** paces to and fro. A silence, then **DE L'ORIENT** sings.

DE L'ORIENT
There is an herb, they say,
Gives light to all the blind.
'Twill be a gracious day
When I that herb shall find.
And lighten all the blind!
There is a leaf that springs.
Will heal the very sad.
Ah, would that I had wings

To find that leaf so glad,
And heal the very sad!
There is a bloom o' grace
Will bring the dead again.
Ah, for the flowret's face!
Ah, for an end to pain!
Ah, for the dead again!

DE VARDES
Why, that's a mournful thing!

DE L'ORIENT
It was so meant.
Oh, happy days we sing the saddest things!—
My heart is eased. I'll sleep awhile and dream.

[He pillows his head upon his arm and sleeps. **DE VARDES** walks slowly to and fro.

DE VARDES
Sleep!—How long has it been since Sleep and I
Met in the heavy road and laid us down,
Took our dear ease, and let the world go by?—
I well remember in the north one time,—
Beside Moselle, where all the live-long day
Upon a stairway old we stood on guard,
De Buc and I, and looked on Mutiny,
Brazen and bold, Death visible and dark!—
And all the night before in council spent,
After a day's forced march from Lunéville,
And a wild night of wine and rapiers drawn.—
As the sun set we heard a bugle blown,
Beat of the drums, and thunder of the guns,
And Bouillé's voice, assurance of relief!—
Another night of council, then at dawn
We slept. The moon was crescent and a star
Shone on to guide the white, enchanted boat
Through seas of ether coloured like a shell;
The trees were dark beneath; there was no sound;
The air was cold,—we laid us down and slept.
Saint Gris! No dreams did trouble us that day!—

[He rests upon the choir step.

To bring the dead again! No flowret blooms,
No herb, no leaf, shall bring the dead again.
No garden is there where for all one's gold,
The weightiest sceptre or the keenest sword,
Might one obtain the happy gardener's place,

And find the bloom that brings the dead again.
It grows not here, and there is naught will serve,
No rain of tears, no delving earnestly,
No lift of hope, no squandered treasury,
Love nor remorse, nor longing nor great pain.
The star has shot. The dead come not again.

[He rises and again walks to and fro.

Happy the dead.—Ah, what of one who lives?
What of that mask in this fantastic dance
Who crowned herself with poison flowers and laughed
To see the lilies fade before her breath?—
O death! O love! O blasting treachery!
O face that in the prison of La Force
Visited my dreams—

[The door opens. **YVETTE** leans against it, panting, then comes forward.

YVETTE
Where is the paper?

DE VARDES
The paper?

YVETTE
The letter to the judges!
Folded and hidden in the purse I sent—

DE VARDES
You sent?—

YVETTE
By Séraphine! You have it, sure?

[She looks about her.

Where is she?—The Citoyenne Blanchefôret?

DE VARDES
She's dead.

YVETTE
No.

DE VARDES
Yes.

YVETTE
All is black before me!

DE VARDES
They called her name—She said adieu and went.
They slew her in the street.

YVETTE
Alas!

DE VARDES
She's dead,
Who was so fair. Why do you say alas?

YVETTE
Too late!—O God, I thought that all was well!

DE VARDES
Why, so it is! With her 'tis well. She's dead.
They say the dead are happy.

YVETTE
You loved her!

DE VARDES
Goddess of Reason, no! Mere friends were we.
But I've a preference for my friends alive!

YVETTE
Oh, woe is me!

DE VARDES
Thou hast what thou didst seek.
Return to Olympus and hear "All hail,
Well done, and like a deity!"

YVETTE
The paper!

DE VARDES
Thou dream of Paimpont Wood!—

YVETTE
The purse of gold!

DE VARDES
Thou picture of the Duchess Jeanne!

YVETTE
The purse!
Give, give!

DE VARDES
The purse!—I gave it to Grégoire.

YVETTE
What!

DE VARDES
It bought five minutes—I did not know
'Twas thine.

YVETTE [To **GRÉGOIRE**]
You did not open it!

DE VARDES
No!

YVETTE
Oh, woe, woe is me!

DE VARDES
Thou standest there!
Still, still the herd girl on the green cliff head
Who waves her hand to a lost boat at sea!
Still, still the vision of a haunted wood
Soulless as is the stone thou leanest on,—
Vivien musing on the thing she's done!

YVETTE
A slip of paper in a silken purse—

DE VARDES
Wilt thou begone? The Mountain waits.

YVETTE
Too late!
Where is Grégoire?

DE VARDES
I know not. He's away;
He has thy gold—I'm sorry for't.

YVETTE
No hope?—
I thought the bridge was built and both were o'er.

Then as I passed I heard "To-morrow morn
Carrier himself will judge that ci-devant"

DE VARDES
The Mountain waits—

YVETTE
I'll to Lalain again.

DE VARDES
Ha!

YVETTE
She is dead; I'm lost. But thou—But thou—
Farewell! Farewell!

DE VARDES
Thou said'st, I'll to Lalain.
I do forbid it utterly.

YVETTE
Oh!

DE VARDES
Obey!
It is thy seigneur's last command.
[To himself]
Thou fool!
Touch not her hand. 'Tis red!

YVETTE
Monseigneur!

DE VARDES
Why art thou both so fair and foul a thing?

YVETTE
Ay, call me that—I care not!

DE VARDES
I'll call thee "Death,
Sweet Death—fair Treachery!"

YVETTE
Forgive, forgive!

DE VARDES
There's blood upon thy hand.

YVETTE
Forgive!

DE VARDES
Alas!
Thou didst betray!

YVETTE
I would that I were dead
In Paimpont Wood, beside the Druid Stone!

DE VARDES
I would that I had never strayed that way!

YVETTE
I won that paper in that purse of gold!
And it was life, I tell thee, life for both!
O God! how all things here miscarry!

DE VARDES
I would that I had never seen thy face!

YVETTE
Oh, much I hated her, la belle Marquise,
And yester morn I did betray her there,
Just in the moment God gave o'er my soul!
And she is dead—I cannot bring her back.
Oh, swift the madness passed and came remorse,
And I did hate myself, and strove to save!—
Oh, woe, and double woe! He promised me!
Oh, I have striven with a fiend from hell
And not prevailed, though sorely I did strive!
O God! O God! I'm weary of the light!
Now, now thou too wilt die unless—unless—
Ah, let me go—Farewell, a little while!

DE VARDES
Not till I know where thou dost go, and why.

YVETTE
Rémond Lalain gave me that paper.
It was an order, written by himself,
Whom even Carrier would not offend—
A secret paper not for every eye.
Reward he asked for certain services,—
Two lives, your life and hers—and hers, I swear!
He does not leave his villa all this day,

But at the judgment bar you were to show
That paper to Lambertye or Sarlat,
And both were saved—both, both, I swear it, both!
And now she's dead—'Twas life you flung away
Shut in that purse! You gave it to Grégoire!
Grégoire! He serves the Revolution,
Is flint to all beside! Oh me! Oh me!
I could not come myself, I could but send.
I won it not till cockcrow of this morn!

DE VARDES
Till cockcrow!

YVETTE
The dawn came slowly on.
The cock crew and I drew the curtain by
And saw the morning star above the Loire!

DE VARDES
The morning star!

YVETTE
'Twas like the eye of God!
I used to watch it from the fields at dawn;
This morn 'twas watching me!

DE VARDES
Rémond Lalain!

YVETTE
'Twas all in vain. She's dead—ah, ages since!
You'll not forgive—So fare you well again!

DE VARDES
Where goest thou, Yvette?

YVETTE
To Séraphine,
Beneath the Lanterne, Sign of the Hour Glass!

DE VARDES
Hear and obey! It is a dying man
Speaks to thee now and with authority!—
Thy seigneur too, and head of all thy house.
When I am dead, the last of the De Vardes
Will be thyself, my cousin!—All song doth say
That Duchess Jeanne who lived so long ago,
Whose pictured face and thine are counterparts,

E'en to the shadowy hair, the cheek's soft curve,
The light of eye, the slow, enchanting smile,—
All song doth say she had a bruisèd heart,
But in God's sight a height of soul! So thou.
Go thou to Morbec. Leave this Babylon.
Back! from the travelled road thy foot's upon!
List not unto the music that is played;
Touch not the scarlet flowers, the honey-sweet,
They'll poison thee! Think not the light is fair,
It is false dawn. Take thou the darkling way
Shall lead thee to white light and lasting bloom!
Go thou to Morbec. Take thy distaff up,
Spin thou thy flax and listen to old tales,
Peacefully, with that smile upon thy lip!
Or in the dewy dawn lift up thy head
From dreamless sleep and drive thy cows afield,
Stand mid the golden broom and mark the mist
Rise from the hidden sea, and hear the lark
Singing afar his strain of heavenly hope,—
So wear thy years away, ah, tranquilly!—
Thou art so young—All this will come to seem
A dream of yesternight—

YVETTE
Dost thou forgive?

DE VARDES
And at the last when Death shall take thy hand,
Smile at the due caress, and lightly come—
If I am I, I'll meet thee on the strand!

YVETTE
Dost thou forgive?

DE VARDES
I love!

YVETTE
Me?

DE VARDES
Thou sayest.

YVETTE
Where is the music playing?

DE VARDES
Long ago,

To Paris and my King I rode away,
Long ago, in the freshness of the world!
I left thee there, all safe in convent fold—
Fair were the fruit trees in that garden old,
Warm shone the sun, the silver fountain played.
I left thee there and thought to find again,
When King and Crown were saved and devoir done,
The battle o'er, the bugles sounding peace!—
The King he is in heaven, the Crown is lost,
The battle's to the strong, the war drum rattles on.
Long lay I in the prison of La Force;
A dream I had that thou wouldst wait for me,
Beside the fountain, by the bright fruit trees.
Thou must have known that bars kept me from thee!
Thou must have known that I did love thee true!
Thou must have known that I did longing wait
The rainbow after storm, the halcyon time
When, stilled the jar and discord of the mind,
The all unfettered heart might speak of love!
But ah, the garden's sealed. Thou art not there!
Thou wouldst not wait the while—

YVETTE
Outside I kneel;
Outside the garden, outside Paradise!
Oh, woe! Oh, bliss!

DE VARDES
Weep not!

YVETTE
I love thee so!

DE VARDES
Paimpont! Paimpont! I feel thy magic wind!

[Re-enter **GRÉGOIRE**.

GRÉGOIRE
Citoyen Vardes—

YVETTE
Grégoire, Grégoire! the purse—
The purse of gold!—

GRÉGOIRE
Hein?

DE VARDES
Let be! Let be!
No purse was there! Dost hear, dost hear, Yvette?
No purse, no gold, no paper, no Lalain!
Thou dost not think that I would take my life?

YVETTE
No!

DE VARDES
Well said, and like the Duchess Jeanne!
Let not Grégoire mistake thee either!

YVETTE
I said I know not what, Grégoire, nor why!
Sometimes a woman says she knows not what.
Why should I talk of purses, faith, now why!

GRÉGOIRE
What do you here, Citoyenne?

YVETTE
I know not.
I strayed this way, a gaoler let me in.
'Tis of the sights of Nantes, this church, this gaol!

GRÉGOIRE [To **DE VARDES**]
I have in charge to guard you through the street
To the old Prison of the Séminaire.
They who lodge there go onward to the Loire!

[He turns to **DE L'ORIENT**.

DE VARDES [To **YVETTE**]
Oh, sunken eyes! Oh, cheek so deadly pale!
Oh, rest thee, rest thee, child, in still Morbec!
Our Lady guard thee, guide thee with her hand.
Farewell—

YVETTE
I'll walk upon the banks of Loire.

DE VARDES
No; come not there!

YVETTE
I must. It is my road.

GRÉGOIRE [He touches **DE L'ORIENT** upon the shoulder]
Awake, poet, and go along with us!

DE L'ORIENT
I am awake! 'Tis trudge again, De Vardes!
Come, Fanchon and Babette,
Olympe and Joséphine!
The dancers all are met
Within the forest green!
Cerise to me,
Denise to thee,
But none to Léontine!

[He turns with **GRÉGOIRE** to the door at left of the altar.

DE VARDES
Farewell—my douce!

YVETTE
Farewell—my fisherman!
Oh—

GRÉGOIRE
Come!

DE L'ORIENT
The dancers all are met
Within the forest green!

[Exeunt **DE VARDES**, **DE L'ORIENT**, and **GRÉGOIRE**. The church darkens. **YVETTE** moves to the choir step.

YVETTE
Oh, love in my heart! Oh, splendour and light!
The bow in the sky, the bird at its height!
The glory and state of the angels bright!

[She kneels and stretches out her arms to the altar.

Oh, mother of sorrows!

CURTAIN

ACT V

SCENE I

A Judgment Hall in Nantes. A dais upon which at a heavy table sit several **MEMBERS** of the Revolutionary Committee. Behind them **SOLDIERS** and a great tricolour flag. To one side a tribune draped with tricolour; opposite the tribune a gallery filled with **WOMEN** of the Revolution. Upon the floor of the hall a throng of red-capped **MEN**. To the right of the dais a number of the accused, **MEN** and **WOMEN**. To the left a small group of the **CONDEMNED**.

Uproar in the hall. An **ACCUSED** who has been standing before the **JUDGES** rejoins the right-hand group of **PRISONERS**. One of the **JUDGES** rings the bell on the table before him.

THE JUDGE
Silence, Citoyennes in the gallery!
You disturb judgment!

CÉLISTE [Leaning from the gallery]
We would know up here
Why you did free that man?

THE JUDGE [Soothingly]
Ah, Citoyenne!
He's not free—he's but acquitted!

CÉLISTE
Ah, well!
That's different!
[To the **WOMEN** about her]
He's but acquitted!

THE **WOMEN** [They nod their heads]
Ah!

[Enter **LALAIN** with **NANON** and **ANGÉLIQUE**.

CÉLISTE
Hé! Angélique! Nanon!

[**NANON** and **ANGÉLIQUE** make their way through the press to the gallery stairs.

THE CROWD
Rémond Lalain.

A JUDGE
Thy place is here, Lalain!

LALAIN
Make way, my friends.
The Levée's thronged to-day.

THE CROWD

Ha, ha, 'tis so!
Levée of the Citoyen Carrier!
Vive la République! Vive Rémond Lalain!

[**LALAIN** sits beside the **JUDGES**.

A JUDGE [To a **GAOLER**]
The next.

THE GAOLER
Dog of a priest!

[**THE ABBÉ** approaches the bar.

THE ABBÉ
On yesterday,
Messieurs the Judges, you acquitted me.

A JUDGE
It is to-day.

THE ABBÉ
Citoyen Lambertye—

LAMBERTYE [Hastily]
I give thee o'er—I give thee o'er—

THE ABBÉ
Parbleu!
Samaritan! Would I had played Levite!
And left thee in the ditch with every wound
Till Satan came to hale his minion forth!—
Well, with this life I've done!

FIRST JUDGE
Thou art a priest

THE ABBÉ
Granted.

SECOND JUDGE
Death!

A TRICOTEUSE [From the gallery]
Hé! Citoyen, below there!
I've dropped my knitting. Throw it here to me!

THIRD JUDGE

Thou hast aided emigrés.

THE ABBÉ
Granted.

SECOND JUDGE
Death!

FIRST JUDGE
And written unto exiles.

THE ABBÉ
Granted.

SECOND JUDGE
Death!

THIRD JUDGE
Thou hast been heard to scorn and to lament
That which the Revolution hath achieved!

THE ABBÉ
Scorn and lament! Why, no, I've wept with joy
To see the things the Revolution hath achieved!
As—

FIRST JUDGE
As what?

THE ABBÉ
Why, thou death's-head, many things!
It did achieve, for one, my brother's death!

THIRD JUDGE
Dost thou mourn for him?

THE ABBÉ
Ay!

SECOND JUDGE
Death!

THE ABBÉ
Achieve! I like the word. Achieve, achieve!
Ruin and downfall, death and waste of fame!
Achievement of the Revolution! Ha,
I'll tell thee, farceur, what it hath achieved:
It hath achieved the death of the Gironde,

Death of Marat, and death of D'Orléans,
Death of great part of its abhorrèd brood!
It hath achieved the Company of Marat;
It hath achieved Jacques Carrier in Nantes;
It shall achieve more death and infamy!
Death! The word you are so fond of. Death!
And Infamy, the thing you can't bestow!
It shall achieve the death of Carrier,
The death of Lambertye and of Lalain,
The death of Danton and of Robespierre!—
Nature will give a grave obscene and dark,
And Time will see that docks and darnels grow!

[Uproar.

THE FIRST JUDGE
Death,—stand aside, condemned.

[Enter **SÉRAPHINE**.

CÉLISTE
Ah, Séraphine,
Come up here, Séraphine!

[**SÉRAPHINE** mounts the stair and sits beside **CÉLISTE**, **ANGÉLIQUE**, and **NANON**.

NANON
Where is Yvette?

SÉRAPHINE
I know not, I!

ANGÉLIQUE
I saw her gliding by,
Beneath the moon, last night when all was still.
Against a cannon in the empty square
She leaned, and on the river looked.

SÉRAPHINE
What harm?

ANGÉLIQUE
Why, none!

CÉLISTE [Her eyes upon the **PRISONERS** below]
Ha, ha! it is the old man's turn!

A GAOLER

Château-Gui!

THE WOMAN
Ah, Château-Gui!

FIRST JUDGE
Château-Gui!

MLLE. DE CHÂTEAU-GUI
O my father!

COUNT LOUIS
Unclasp thy hands, my child!
What is it, Lambertye?

FIRST JUDGE
Thou ci-devant,
Thou art accused, imprimatur, of this:
Once thou didst serve Capet!

COUNT LOUIS
The King?

FIRST JUDGE
Capet.

COUNT LOUIS
I served the King of France.

FIRST JUDGE
Twice over, death! For thou didst serve Capet;
For thou dost dare say the King of France!

COUNT LOUIS
The King of France!

THE CROWD
Ah!—

COUNT LOUIS
Son of Saint Louis!

THE CROWD
Ah!—

COUNT LOUIS
Royal Martyr!

THE CROWD
Ah—h—h.

MLLE. DE CHÂTEAU-GUI
O my father!

THIRDJUDGE
All titles, terms of honour and of state,
Majesty and reverence are forbid,
Not to be spoken! They are ci-devants,
They are condemned.

THE CROWD
Condemned!

COUNT LOUIS
Ha, ci-devants,
Titles and symbols, names and attributes,
Condemned for splendour and for high estate!
Ha, Croix de Saint Louis! Ha, Château-Gui!
Thou goest to heaven in famous company:
King, Saint, Martyr, Reverence, Majesty.—
Best make the company a regiment—
Regiment du Roi, in vestments gorgeous!
Forbidden words! Who says to me "forbid"?
Ye sans-culottes, ye bourgeois, creeping things,
Adders and asps that slew a king and queen!
I am a courtier of the olden time
Who served le Grand Monarque, knew Mazarin,
And in a Court shall still be courtier,
Croix de Saint Louis, with the grande entrée,
While ye do prowl in filthy ways of hell,
Nor hardly see its red-lit Œil-de-bœuf
Where everlasting Terror, groaning, reigns,—
But, being lackeys, keep the lackeys' place!

FIRST JUDGE
Enough!

SECOND JUDGE
Death!

THE CROWD
Death! The Loire!

COUNT LOUIS
O Kings of France!
O sons of Clovis and of Charlemagne!

Louis the Pious and the Debonair!
Philippe August and Fair, and Charles the Wise!
And thou the sainted King, the Blessed Louis!
And Charles Bien-Aimé, Victorieux,
Crowned by the maiden of Domrémy!
And the good King Henri, Henri the Great!
Louis the Just, Louis le Grand Monarque!
Louis the Loved, and Louis lately dead,
The Martyr King, the Martyr, Martyr King!—
O Kings of France in that fair land ye be,
To your châteaux and to your palaces
Prepare to welcome dying loyalty!
For knightly faith is marching forth from France.
Throne, sceptre, orb, and majesty have passed,
Ermine and coronet and spur of gold,
Renown and splendid honour, valiant sway,
Ancien Régime, noblesse of old France!
The oriflamme upon its golden stem,
The banner of the lilies waving high!—

THE CROWD
Ah—

COUNT LOUIS
The lily banner and the oriflamme!
Forgotten yonder stripes of shame and woe!

THE CROWD
The tricolour! Death! The Loire!

FIRST JUDGE
Death to-night!

COUNT LOUIS
Nightshade, mandrake, and hemlock o'er ye wave!—
But I am going where, I make no doubt,
The favourite flower is still the fleur-de-lis!

THE CROWD
Ah!

COUNT LOUIS
And the word forbid is république!

THE CROWD
Down! down!

COUNT LOUIS

Princes and peers of France!

FIRST JUDGE
Have done!

COUNT LOUIS
Anjou, Lorraine!

THE CROWD
Ah—h—h!

COUNT LOUIS
Bourbon and Valois!

[Uproar in the hall. **MLLE. DE CHÂTEAU-GUI** clings to her father's arm.

Forbidden words! Well, well, my child, I'm done!
My breath is out.—Forbidden words! Ma foi!
'Tis to my taste to deal in contraband!

[The **FIRST JUDGE** rings the bell violently. The tumult subsides.

A GAOLER
Château-Gui, take place beside the priest!

THE ABBÉ
Ah,
Monsieur le Comte!

COUNT LOUIS
Monsieur l'Abbé!

[He offers his snuff-box.

FIRST JUDGE
The next.

[Enter **YVETTE**. The **CROWD** murmurs as it makes way.

THE CROWD
Yvette Charruel!

A MAN
Goddess of Reason!

[**YVETTE** mounts the stair to the gallery and sits beside **SÉRAPHINE**.

CÉLISTE

So pale!

ANGÉLIQUE
No rose?

NANON
Only her lips are red.

CÉLISTE
So heavy-eyed?

YVETTE
I have not slept.

A YOUNG GIRL [Near her]
Oh, oh,
Thy voice! 'Tis like a violin playing!

ANGÉLIQUE
I know thou didst not sleep.—How looked the Loire
Beneath the moon last night?

YVETTE
Much as 'twill look
Beneath the moon to-night.

[With her chin upon her hand she studies the throng below.

SÉRAPHINE
The prisoners—

YVETTE
Who rises there?

FIRST JUDGE
Thou ci-devant, De Vardes!

THE CROWD
De Vardes! De Vardes! Aristocrat! De Vardes!

DE VARDES
Rémond Lalain—

LALAIN
René de Vardes.

DE VARDES
This court—

Pray you conceive it is some greensward trim,
My cartel sent, received, the duel fought,
And thou the victor, since so wags the world,
Heart's blood of mine upon thy rapier dark!
And I the vanquished in the sight of men,
Drowsing to death upon the bloody sod.
And all this folk but seconds, witnesses,
They are not here, nor there; we are the men!
Now, seeing death hath some prerogative,
I charge thee stand, antagonist! nor leave
This sunny field with thy triumphant friends
Until I bid thee go!

LALAIN
I hear!
[To the **CROWD**]
Silence!

DE VARDES
When I do think that once I called thee friend,
My wonder grows! The orchard's blooming now
Where we did lie at length on summer eves
The while the mavis sang and sea winds blew,
And to the nodding clover droned the bee,—
Two striplings couched beneath an apple tree,
Talking of knights at arms and paladins
And what we each would dare in worthy cause!
That brow of thine was not so swarthy then,
Thine eyes were frank, we read from the same book
The deeds of Palmerin and Amadis.
Then up we lightly rose and went our way,
Hand touching hand,—Orestes, Pylades!
I, Jonathan the Prince, and David thou!
The figure holds, for Jonathan will die,
But wilt thou mourn him, David? No, I say!—
Nor o'er his kingdom shalt thou reign, Rémond!

LALAIN
René—

DE VARDES
I am, monsieur, the Baron of Morbec!

THE CROWD
Ah!

LALAIN
Silence!

[To **DE VARDES**]
As thou wilt! He is long dead
That youth thou namest David.

DE VARDES
Ay, Citoyen,
He slew himself. I see his punishment.

LALAIN
Oh!—

DE VARDES
Wretched man! What hast thou done? I know,
And thou, Rémond, dost know I know! Enough.
O better far to lie upon this sod
And hear the wings of death above my head,
Than to be thou, thou stainèd conqueror!
Dishonoured thou from helm to bloody heel!
Enough! When the cock crows and the morning star
Shines steadfast over Loire I shall be gone.
One stays, that's God. Do thou beware, Rémond,
For God will hearken unto Jonathan—
Thou canst not hurt a flower that he loved!

LALAIN
No?

DE VARDES
No!

LALAIN
Thou mightst have had thy life—

DE VARDES
I?

[He laughs.

YVETTE
Air!
You hem me in, Citoyennes! Air! De grâce!

NANON
The air is good enough for us, Yvette!

ANGÉLIQUE
Why do you grow so pale, so pale, Yvette?

[**YVETTE** takes from her hair the bonnet-rouge.

SÉRAPHINE
Psst! Little fool! Put on the cap again!

YVETTE
It is too heavy!

SÉRAPHINE
Saint Yves! Put it on!

DE VARDES
The duel's o'er; the night is drawing on;
Dark is thy form against the crimson sky,
Rémond Lalain! Stand further off, my foe!
And now I think I see thee not at all,
And that is well! I would forget thee quite.
Live out thy life unto its sordid close!
Live on, and in the future find the past!
But while thou treadest earth touch not again
That flower I spoke of! Touch it not, Lalain!

LALAIN
Draws on the night—

DE VARDES
I'll bathe me in the Loire!
Death has been ever called a River wide.
This ford I fear not!—Soldier of the King,
I'll pass the stream, though cold, though cold and dark!
The bivouac lights are shining through the trees,
He waits within my tent, my General!

FIRST JUDGE
Death!

SECOND JUDGE
Death!

DE VARDES
Now sheath thy sword, Rémond!
The field of honour leave to death and me!

[He crosses to the condemned.

COUNT LOUIS
Monsieur le Baron!

THE ABBÉ
René de Vardes!

DE VARDES
Monsieur le Comte, Monsieur l'Abbé, again
I find myself in best of company!

[The **JUDGES** whisper together. **LALAIN**, his eyes upon the floor, drums upon the table with his hand.

[**YVETTE** unpins the tricolour cockade from her breast, gazes upon it for a moment, then throws it from her. The women about her watch her greedily.

SÉRAPHINE
Name of a name! Yvette!

YVETTE
I like white best.

SÉRAPHINE
Saint Gildas! Saint Maudez!

YVETTE
I ever loved
The fleur-de-lis!

SÉRAPHINE
Saint Yves le Véridique!

YVETTE [She rises]
God and the King!

[Uproar in the hall. **ALL** turn toward the gallery.

A JUDGE
Who cried that?

A BRETON SAILOR
Sainte Vierge!
Yvette Charruel!

LALAIN
No!

DE VARDES
Mon Dieu!

THE CROWD
Yvette—

Yvette Charruel!

SÉRAPHINE
Saint Servan! Saint Linaire!

YVETTE
I denounce the Citoyen Rémond Lalain!

THE CROWD
Ah!—

NANON
Ah, let me get at her!

LALAIN
Citoyens!
Heed her not—she's mad!—The next prisoner!

YVETTE
I denounce Carrier and Lambertye!
Chicanneau, Sarlat, Petit-Pierre, and Gaye,
The Company of Marat, the hideous deaths,
The Noyades and the Dragonades of Nantes!
I tell you that the blood you shed must stop!
One cannot sleep at night with thinking on't.
You put to sleep, O God! too many!

THE CROWD
Ah!—

A VOICE
There is no God! nor ever was in Nantes!

ANOTHER VOICE
She has spoken against the Republic!

YVETTE
There was a glory in the morning sky,
Where now is naught but miserable red!
A trumpet blew, but we have listened since
To the false jingle of a tambourine!
There stood a mighty judge, robed, calm and proud,
Where is he now? I see but murderers!

A VOICE
But murderers!

YVETTE

I denounce the Republic!

[Uproar.

THE CROWD
Oh, harlotry!—No, blasphemy!—Down, down!
The Bar! the Judgment Bar!—The river!—Death!
The Loire!

YVETTE
I am coming.

[She descends the stair. **MEN** and **WOMEN** clutch her and thrust her forward to the bar.

I am here!
I am Yvette, called Right of the Seigneur.
My mother was the peasant girl, Yvonne;
My father was the Baron of Morbec.
I am tired of Ça ira, Carmagnole,
I would sleep with the Loire for my pillow!

THE CROWD
Ah—h—h!

LALAIN
A head beside thine on that pillow!

DE VARDES
Mon Dieu!

YVETTE
Perhaps, Citoyen!

A VOICE
I denounce
Yvette Charruel!

OTHER VOICES
And I!—And I!—And I!

CURTAIN

SCENE II

The banks of the Loire. Night. Branching trees; between their trunks is seen the river. There is a full moon, but a drifting mist obscures the scene. In the background, upon the river bank, dimly appears a **CROWD** of the condemned, **MEN**, **WOMEN**, and **CHILDREN**, **SOLDIERS** and **EXECUTIONERS** of the

Company of Marat. From this throng comes a low, continued, confused sound of command, entreaty, distress, and lamentation. In the foreground the condemned form into **GROUPS** or move singly to and fro.

Enter **YVETTE** from the shadow of the trees.

A SOLDIER [Following her]
Holà! Give us not the slip!

YVETTE
Thou soldier!
There is no gold could make me flee this place!
How long dost think before they throw me in?
The Soldier
A little while!

[He returns to the river. **YVETTE** sits upon the earth at the foot of a tree, and with her chin upon her hand watches those who come and go.

YVETTE
He comes not yet! O Our Lady!
I would not drown till I have seen him once!

A WOMAN [Passing with a **MAN**]
How shines the moon! Did we not always say,
We two would die by such a moon as this?
Rememberest thou—

THE MAN
Rememberest thou that night,
That Versailles night within the Orangerie?

THE WOMAN
Rememberest thou—

[They pass.

A SOLDIER [Calling to another]
To bind them hand and foot,
We need more rope!

THE SECOND SOLDIER
Just thrust them in the stream
With bayonets!
A Cry from the River
Miséricorde!

[**A CHILD** with flowers in her hand speaks to **YVETTE**.

THE CHILD
I'm tired—

YVETTE
Rest here, thou little bird!

THE CHILD
My name's Aimée.
I did not know that flowers grew at night.
Is that the moon?

YVETTE
It is the silver moon!
Aimée's a pretty name. My name's Yvette.

THE CHILD
Kiss me, Yvette—I'll look now for Ursule!

YVETTE
Who is Ursule?

THE CHILD
My bonne—Adieu, Yvette!

[The **CHILD** passes on.

VOICES FROM THE RIVER
Hélas! Hélas! Miséricorde!

[A **NUN** advances from the shadow. She is in ecstasy, her hands clasped, her eyes raised.

THE NUN
The skies open: heaven appears!
Heaven my home!
O for the wings of the dove,
The eagle's speed!
The gates of pearl are opening,
My harp is strung.
The Virgins come to meet me.
Sainte Agnès, Sainte Claire!
Our Lady stoops to greet me.
My father smiles.
My brothers two I see there!
Who is that one
Who kneels and to me beckons?
'Tis he I loved!
What radiance grows, what splendour?

Who waiting stands?
Light! O Light! O Christ my Lord!
Heaven my home!
O Love! O Death, come quickly!
I would be gone!

[A **SOLDIER** touches her on the arm.

THE SOLDIER
Thy time it is!

[The **NUN** regards him with a radiant and dazzling smile, then turns and moves swiftly before him to the river.

THE VOICES
Woe, woe! Miséricorde!

YVETTE
Heaven my home! Shall I see heaven then?
Oh me! so much of ill thou'st done, Yvette!
Alas! Alas! What if I cannot win
To heaven! but must ever weeping stand
With all the lost and strain my eyes to see
The form I love move 'neath the living trees,
And all in vain, so great the distance is!—
Not see him! O Our Lady, let me in!

THE VOICES
Woe, woe!—I die!—I die!—O countrymen!

YVETTE
O God, and is it true I murdered her,
That lady high, that fair, so fair Clarice?
O God! I would that she were happy here,
Alive and laughing, gay of heart again!
O God! I do repent me of my sin!

THE VOICES
Ayez pitié!

[From a group of **THE CONDEMNED** is heard the voice of **THE ABBÉ**.

THE ABBÉ
Miserere mei Deus
Secundum magnam misericordiam tuam!

THE CONDEMNED [Kneeling]
Have mercy, O God!

VOICES FROM THE RIVER
Miséricorde!

[**YVETTE** kneels.

THE ABBÉ
In manus tuas Domine commendo spiritum meum,
Redemisti me Domine Deus veritatis!

THE CONDEMNED
O God, receive our souls!

VOICES FROM THE RIVER
Woe, woe! We die!

SOLDIERS
That one is swimming there! Your musket! Fire!—

[A musket shot.

Ha, ha! Ha, ha!

THE ABBÉ
Dulcissime Domine Jesu Christe,
Per virtutem sanctissimae Passionis tuae
Recipe me in numerum electorum tuorum!

THE CONDEMNED
O Christ, receive our souls! O Christ who died!

THE ABBÉ
Maria, Mater gratiae, Mater misercordiae,
Tu me ab hoste protege, et hora mortis suscipe!

THE CONDEMNED
O mother of God!

VOICES
Miséricorde!

THE ABBÉ
Omnes sancti Angeli, et omnes Sancti
Intercedite pro me, et mihi succurrite!

VOICES
Miséricorde!

SOLDIERS
Petit-Pierre!—André!
'Tis time for yonder folk beneath the trees!

THE ABBÉ
Ego te absolvo a peccatis tuis,
In nomine Patris, et Filii, et Spiritus Sancti.
Amen!

[**THE CONDEMNED** arise from their knees.

THE SOLDIERS
Come your ways!

[**THE ABBÉ** and the condemned vanish into the mist upon the river bank.

VOICES
Ayez pitié!

[**YVETTE** rises from her knees. She plucks the yellow broom that grows beneath the trees.

YVETTE
And if I may I will her servant be,
And I will bring her posies every day!

THE VOICES
We die!

SOLDIERS
So, two and two! Ha, ha!

[There appears in mid-stream on the river Carrier's festal barge. It is lit from stem to stern. There is music aboard, singing and revelry of **MEN** and **WOMEN**.

LAUGHTER FROM THE RIVER
Ha, ha! Ha, ha! Ha, ha!

THE VOICES
They laugh! They sing!

[A sound of singing from the passing barge.

A WOMAN'S VOICE
Fair Chloris bathed her in the flood,
Young Damon watching, trembling stood,
Behind the frailest hawthorn wall!
The month was May—

A MAN'S VOICE
No, Prairial!

THE WOMAN'S VOICE
Her ivory limbs they gleamed and turned,
Young Damon's heart so hotly burned,
Into the stream he leaped therefor!
It seemed July—

THE MAN'S VOICE
No, Thermidor!

[The barge passes.

VOICES FROM THE RIVER
O hearts so hard!

OTHER VOICES
Oh, woe! Adieu! Adieu!

[An **OLD WOMAN** speaks to **YVETTE**.

THE OLD WOMAN
They've drowned my son, my sailor son Michel!
Oh, oh, my heart! he's drifting out to sea!

YVETTE
Poor mother!

THE OLD WOMAN
Oh, to and fro he sailed, he sailed!
The Indies knew him and the Northern Seas!
He'd bide at home a bit, then off he'd go,
Another voyage make, strange things to see!
Then home he'd come and of his travels tell.
Oh, oh, my son, my sailor son Michel!

[The **OLD WOMAN** passes on.

[Enter **SÉRAPHINE**.

SÉRAPHINE
I've sought her here, I've sought her there, in vain!
And perilous it is to seek one here!

YVETTE
Séraphine!

SÉRAPHINE
Yvette!

YVETTE
Where is monseigneur?

SÉRAPHINE [Weeping]
I know not, I!—Saint Lazaire and Saint Jean!
I nursed thee ere thou wast so high!

YVETTE
Poor Séraphine! Dear Séraphine!

SÉRAPHINE
Alack!
They're watching there!

YVETTE
Oh, then away!
'Tis death to weep for one who dies! Away!

SÉRAPHINE [Weeping]
Oh, oh! When thou wast but a little thing
Thou hadst the coaxing ways! Alack! Alack!

YVETTE
Poor Séraphine!

SÉRAPHINE
Dost mind the sunny path
Up the steep cliff to chapel in the woods?

YVETTE
I mind—I mind—To thy warm hand I clung,
A little child. Now I must walk alone!

SÉRAPHINE
Oh, oh! And thou wast Goddess yesterday,
The fairest Goddess ever seen, they say!

YVETTE
Speak not of that!

A VOICE [Calling]
Séraphine! Séraphine!

YVETTE
It warns, that voice! Adieu, adieu, adieu!

Thou must begone!

SÉRAPHINE
If I do look at thee
I'll stay forever here! Adieu! Adieu!—
Oh well-a-day! Oh well, oh well-a-day!

[Exit **SÉRAPHINE**.

YVETTE
So late it grows, so long I've waited here!
I feel the morning air!—Will he not come?
O God! what if they've slain him otherwhere?
Ha! Death is busy far and near to-night!
They may have shot him yonder by the sea!
He may have sunk above, below this place!
Though Grégoire swore to me it would be here,
Here where they brought me would they bring him too,
And ere the set of moon we would be gone!—
O God! The cries of drowning men I've heard,
But not his voice among them! No, no, no!
He'll make no moan, he will die loftily!—
Ah, God! only to see him ere I drown!

THE VOICES
Miséricorde!

SOLDIERS
Prenez garde! Halte là!

A MAN'S VOICE
I die who fought for France in bloody fields;
At Lille I fought, at Bordeaux, Avignon!

YVETTE
A soldier!

[Another **VOICE** sings hoarsely.

THE VOICE
Tremblez, tyrans! et vous perfides,
L'opprobre de tous les partis!
Tremblez, vos projets parricides
Viennent enfin recevoir leur prix!
Tout est soldat pour vous combattre—

[The **VOICE** dies.

YVETTE
A soldier!

ANOTHER VOICE
Diantre! A whiff of grapeshot now,
A sabre-cut, or e'en a trampling charge!
But this cold death—

[The **VOICE** dies.

YVETTE
A soldier!

ANOTHER VOICE
Baste! I'll tell
The Duc de Biron—

YVETTE
All soldiers!

[Enter **DE VARDES** and **GRÉGOIRE**.

GRÉGOIRE
I tell you truth, monsieur—

DE VARDES
So dense the throng
I have looked up and down for this long hour,—
This hour so long, this hour so fatal short,
Seeing it is my latest hour of life,
And that I cannot find her whom I seek!

GRÉGOIRE
She is not dead, monsieur!

DE VARDES
So many are!

GRÉGOIRE
I would have known.

DE VARDES
Some æons past thou wast
A serviceable fellow! Get thee gone!
And if thou findest her, I'll give thee thanks,
I have no gold—

GRÉGOIRE

Monsieur le Baron—

DE VARDES
Go!

[Exit **GRÉGOIRE**.

And if I find her not, if time shall fail,
Then through thy labyrinth, Eternity,
Love's silken clue shall lead me safe at last—

YVETTE
Monseigneur!

[**DE VARDES** turns.

DE VARDES
Yvette!

[**TWO SOLDIERS** of the Company of Marat pass beneath the trees.

THE FIRST SOLDIER
'Tis near the cockcrow!
What devil's work we've had, and have!

THE SECOND SOLDIER
Courage!
There are not so many now! Then home and sleep!

[They pass.

DE VARDES
Oh, rest thee on thy lover's breast, my heart!
My life, my love, my dear, my Duchess Jeanne!
Oh, 'neath the moon thou'rt like a lily flower!

YVETTE
René, René!

DE VARDES
Thy lips!

[They kiss.

No, no, thou'rt not
That Vivien whom I did call thee once.
She was an evil fay; thou'rt pure and good!
Nor art thou that fair piteous Duchess Jeanne

Who died for love, whose look thou wearest now!
Thou never wast that woman star-begirt,
Whom they did hail as Goddess here in Nantes.
No Goddess thou, thou wan and broken flower!—
This is green Morbec, thou'rt the herd girl there
And I thy fisher, home from out the west.
My heart, my love, my silver rose, my douce!

YVETTE
The flowers drifting from the fragrant trees!
Unearthly light—

[They kiss.

DE VARDES
Now come, Eternity!

VOICES FROM THE RIVER
It is so sad to die!—No, no, 'tis sweet!
Adieu, adieu!

SOLDIERS
So, down! Ha, ha! Les Noces
Républicaines!

DE VARDES
Les Noces Républicaines!

YVETTE
'Tis what they call this death—

SOLDIERS
So near the dawn!
Here are the tricoteuses.

VOICES OF WOMEN
Not yet they've done!
Diantre! So many weddings in one night!
Here are the girls from Carrier's barge at last!

OTHER VOICES
Petit-Pierre! André!

SOLDIERS
Céleste—Nanon!
Zephine, 'Toinette!

THE WOMEN

Vive le son! vive le son!
Dansons la Carmagnole!

A TRICOTEUSE
'Tis light enough to knit! I'll sit me down.
Fi! how the grass is trampled here!

A SOLDIER
Lalain and Lambertye—

A WOMAN
We left them there
Upon the barge, Lalain and Lambertye;
And they were drinking deep, and dicing too,
And Lalain had his arm round Angélique!

[They laugh.

DE VARDES
Seest thou not through yonder trees the stone,
The Druid Stone where I did see thee first
When thou didst lie asleep upon the grass?
How long I stood and looked, thou dost not know!

YVETTE
Beside the stream I slept and dreamed of thee!
I knew it not, but sure I dreamed of thee,
For in my sleep I thought I saw a king!

DE VARDES
O love!—

YVETTE
It is Morbec arises there!
The sands that stretch above the idle waves,
And all the little shells upon the shore!

DE VARDES
The convent bell is ringing! Seest thou not
The fountain old, the fruit trees in the sun?

YVETTE
Oh, life was never made for happiness!
The hour's too short, the wine spills from the cup,
The blossom's shaken ere we know 'tis sweet!

VOICES FROM THE RIVER
Miséricorde!

A SOLDIER
Those two have waited long!
Hi! Petit-Pierre, 'tis time to marry them—

DE VARDES
This Saint John's Eve we'll walk in other woods!
And we will find and name a castle fair,
And rose and heartsease we will plant thereby!
Here ends this road, but we must onward go.
There is a longer hour, a deeper cup!
The blossom's gone, but we shall see the fruit.
And life was made for happiness, my douce!

A VOICE FROM THE RIVER
Mourir pour la patrie,
Mourir pour la France.

DE VARDES
It is a hymn of Chénier's.—France! France!
Not since the days of Clovis hast thou lacked
Strong sons to die for thee, thou Lioness!
But now thy own brood hast thou eaten up,
And in the desert shalt thou roar alone,
Seeing the hunters nearer, nearer creep!
They'll snare thee fast, they'll make of thee a show!
France, France!—and yet thy sons shall ransom thee!

A SOLDIER
A length of rope, André!

ANOTHER
Petit-Pierre—

YVETTE
They come!

DE VARDES
I will go first.

YVETTE
'Tis not their way!
They'll bind us fast together, throw us in
Bound fast together—

DE VARDES
Is it so? Why, then
We are together still, my heart, my life!

We will not struggle as we sink to rest.

A SOLDIER
Man and woman, come your ways!

SECOND SOLDIER
The river
Waits, your marriage bed is spread!

[The knitting **WOMEN** sing from the river bank.

THE WOMEN
We are the tricoteuses!
Our wool we knit beneath the sun and moon!
Knit! knit! knitting every one!
We are the tricoteuses!
The skein we knit is ravelled out full soon!
Knit! knit! the knitting now is done!

YVETTE
The light is growing in the east! My heart
It is so full I cannot speak to thee!

DE VARDES
Put thou thine arms about my neck, Yvette,
And lay thy head upon thy lover's heart,
And veil thine eyes with all thy shadowy hair.
Now let them bind us with what cords they will,
The spirit moves unbound, triumphant, free,
Not through the Loire, but through a vaster stream!
Oh, it is something dimly great to die!
And then to die together, is't not sweet?
And not through illness, age, decrepitude,
But the armed man is ready for new wars.
And thou—

YVETTE
I hear the lark!

A SOLDIER
Come, come away!

[**YVETTE** and **DE VARDES** move together towards the river, into the mist and the shadow of the trees.

A VOICE FROM THE RIVER
Vive la République!

Mary Johnston – A Concise Bibliography

Prisoners of Hope (1898)
By Order of the Company (1900)
To Have and to Hold (1900)
Audrey (1902)
Pioneers of the Old South (1903)
Sir Mortimer (1904)
The Goddess of Reason (1907)
Lewis Rand (1908)
The Long Roll (1911)
Cease Firing (1912)
Hagar (1913)
The Witch (1914)
The Fortunes of Garin (1915)
The Wanderers (1917)
Foes (1918)
Michael Forth (1919)
Sweet Rocket (1920)
Silver Cross (1921)
1492 (1922)
The Great Valley (1926)
The Exile (1927)
Miss Delicia Allen (1932)

Film Adaptations

Audrey (1916)
To Have and to Hold (1916 and in 1922)
Pioneers of the Old South was adapted as the film Jamestown (1923)

www.ingramcontent.com/pod-product-compliance
Lightning Source LLC
LaVergne TN
LVHW050958080826
845145LV00009B/2349

* 9 7 8 1 8 3 9 6 7 5 2 5 6 *